PRESENTED TO:

FROM:

DATE:

# grace not Perfection

FOR YOUNG READERS

*Believing You're Enough in a World of Impossible Expectations*

EMILY LEY

ADAPTED BY TAMA FORTNER

THOMAS NELSON
*Since 1798*

*Grace, Not Perfection for Young Readers*



Tommy Nelson, PO Box 141000, Nashville, TN 37214



Published in Nashville, Tennessee, by Tommy Nelson. Tommy Nelson is an imprint of Thomas Nelson. Thomas Nelson is a registered trademark of HarperCollins Christian Publishing, Inc.

Published in association with Folio Literary Management LLC, 630 Ninth Avenue, Suite 1101, New York, New York 10036.

The writer is represented by Cyle Young of C.Y.L.E. (Cyle Young Literary Elite, LLC), a literary agency.

Tommy Nelson titles may be purchased in bulk for educational, business, fund-raising, or sales promotional use. For information, please e-mail SpecialMarkets@ThomasNelson.com.



ISBN 978-1-4002-1994-0 (audio)
ISBN 978-1-4002-1990-2 (eBook)

**Library of Congress Cataloging-in-Publication Data is on file.**

ISBN 978-1-4002-2001-4

Adapted by Tama Fortner
Unless otherwise noted, photography © Ashley Cochrane Photography.
Images on pages 68, 133, and 134 © Stocksy.

*Printed in China*

20 21 22 23 24 DSC 6 5 4 3 2 1

Mfr: DSC / Dongguan, China / July 2020 / PO #9586533

*To Brady, Tyler, and Caroline—*

*be still and know.*

*You are deeply loved just as you are.*

# CONTENTS

## PART 3: THE GRACE TO BE YOU

# INTRODUCTION

I'M SO GLAD MY BOOK FOUND ITS WAY INTO YOUR hands. I can imagine all the things that you're trying to do. After all, I was once your age. This is a time in your life when you're learning, changing, growing—not only in your body but in your mind and heart and the way you look at the world. It's really exciting!

I bet you feel like you're already juggling so many activities and responsibilities. Some days you probably feel like you're running round and round on a hamster wheel—going as fast as you can, trying to do it all, but feeling like you're getting nowhere. It's an exhausting place to be. I understand. I lived it when I was your age, and I'm still living it. My activities and responsibilities have changed a bit as I've gotten married, had children of my own, and started a business. But trust me, there are days when I still find myself facing that hamster wheel.

I know how fast and overwhelming life can be when you want it *all* and you want to do it all perfectly. I know those aches of your heart. You are probably being pulled in ten different directions, and you might be searching for a little relief. I want to show you how to let go of this whole idea that you have to be perfect in order to be somebody. And I want to show you how to give yourself some grace.

GIVE YOURSELF SOME GRACE.

Let's pretend we're having a chat while sharing a sundae at your favorite ice cream shop. I'll share my journey with you and give you some tips I've learned along the way. But this book isn't about me. This book is about *you*. It's about discovering who you really are and what you really want from this amazing life you've been given. I am so honored to share my journey with you. It's not a perfect one—no one's is. But looking back, I can see God working through every failure and every triumph to create a journey full of joy and peace.

As a designer, I am very concerned with image and making sure everything looks perfect. And I know that habit spills over into my life when I get home. I know what the chase to "have it all together" does to a girl who has big dreams and simply wants to be the best she can be. And I've learned (by falling on my face quite a few times) that being perfect isn't really all it's cracked up to be. Real life—with all its imperfections—feels so much better.

Throughout these pages, we'll explore what it means to give grace to yourself and grace to the people in your life. Together, we'll take a look at steps you can take to set yourself free from chasing perfection. We'll walk through some checklists, questions, and tips for getting things done. We'll dig into the struggles we all face as we try to be our best and make everyone happy. And lastly, we'll explore what it means to discover your true calling—who God created you to be. Together, let's figure out how you can be your best, most real, most joyful self. In a world that expects us to be perfect all the time, you can find something better: you can find grace.

> BEING PERFECT ISN'T REALLY ALL IT'S CRACKED UP TO BE.

*Part 1*

# GIVE YOURSELF SOME GRACE

SOMEWHERE ALONG THE WAY, WE GOT THIS IDEA THAT we have to be perfect. That we aren't good enough just the way we are. We aren't pretty enough, talented enough, or popular enough.

Whether through social media, YouTube, the movies, or other people, we've allowed someone else to tell us who and what and how we should be. That we should be, in a word, *perfect*. We take all the best moments of other people's lives and mash them together to create this image—and then we spend our days trying to live up to that perfect image. We tell ourselves, *If I'm perfect, I'll be good enough. If I'm perfect,*

*I'll fit in. If I'm perfect, I'll finally make everyone happy.* The trouble is that perfection isn't possible.

Every outfit and every activity is held up for inspection: Is it picture-perfect? Is it Instagram-worthy? We measure our worth by the size of our jeans. And busyness? Well, that's just the norm. We run from activity to activity on too little sleep. If we're not doing everything, then we're not doing enough. At least that's what we tell ourselves. So we try to do it all: We make the grades and make the team. We text and Snapchat. We try out and sign up. We overload ourselves, overcommit our time, overwork our minds and bodies, and end up overwhelmed. We try to make everyone happy—except maybe ourselves. And while chasing perfection may (or may not!) earn us lots of "likes" and "friends," it also leaves us feeling empty, alone, and just plain not good enough.

> THE GOOD LIFE IS RICH, REAL, AND SO NOT PERFECT AT ALL.

Without even realizing it, many of us have decided to let the world tell us what the "good life" looks like. And, sweet girl, this isn't it. That picture-perfect life on social media isn't real, and it doesn't equal happiness. Happiness isn't found in having more followers or getting more likes. True joy isn't found in chasing after perfection. The good life is rich, real, and so not perfect at all.

Forget what the world is telling you. You don't have to be more than who you are. *You are enough.* Just the way

God made you. You are worthy of happiness. You deserve heart-bursting joy, belly laughs, and sweet memories of these growing-up years. And you can have that—right where you are, just as you are, with what you have right now. You and I together, through these next few chapters, are going to talk through some simple, *tactical* ways to find this joy.

---

**TACTICAL:** *A specific plan that is created to achieve a particular goal*[1]

---

**YOU**

*are*

**ENOUGH.**

*Chapter 1*

# LET'S TALK ABOUT GRACE

*You have been saved by grace through believing. You did not save yourselves; it was a gift from God.*

EPHESIANS 2:8 NCV

BECAUSE WE'RE GOING TO BE TALKING A LOT ABOUT grace, the first thing we need to do is define what *grace* is. Grace is a gift. It's a gift from God, and it's a gift you can give yourself. God's grace means that He will give you good things because He loves you, not because you've earned them. And to give yourself grace is to accept all the good things He is pouring into your life—even though you aren't perfect. To put it simply, grace is letting go of that impossible-to-reach standard of perfection. It's knowing that you are enough—just as you are—simply because you are God's own amazing creation. And it's trusting that the One who loves you endlessly is still working on you. Sweet girl, you don't have to be perfect to earn God's love. You just have to be you.

> YOU DON'T HAVE TO BE PERFECT TO EARN GOD'S LOVE. YOU JUST HAVE TO BE YOU.

It took me a long time to learn these truths about grace. I wish I had known them when I was your age. But it wasn't until I had everything I thought I needed to make my life perfect—the husband, the family, the home, the business—that I realized how important grace is. Because everything wasn't perfect. The home had to be cared for. The business took so much time and energy. And our sweet little baby boy didn't sleep. *At all.* Life was rich and full and beautiful . . . and exhausting. And that is when I began to learn about grace.

Have you ever gotten everything you thought you needed for your life to be perfect—only to realize those are the very things causing you stress? Maybe you made the team, but the practices are so hard to juggle with the rest of your responsibilities. Or you landed your dream part in the play only to struggle to remember all the lines. Or perhaps you were invited to lunch at the "popular" table only to discover how much work it is to keep fitting in. If that's where you are, then it's time for you to learn about grace too.

## GRACE

I tried for a long time to be the picture-perfect girl with the picture-perfect life. I wanted the world to know I had it all together and it was easy for me. I wanted to be the girl people pointed out and said, "Did you see that super-cute outfit she wore?" or "Did you see that award she won?" To me, that translated to "Did you see how amazing she is?" It's so easy to get caught up in trying to get approval from others. Every "like" becomes another reason to think, *I must be okay—people I don't know very well approve of me and admire me.*

That is a terrible and harmful way of thinking. Too many of us try to prove our worth by wearing the perfect clothes, being on the right teams, and having the right friends. We think if we do everything perfectly then we'll earn the love and admiration of friends, of family, and of God.

When I was growing up, to me, *perfect* meant my parents were proud. *Perfect* meant my teachers and coaches were pleased. *Perfect* meant popular. *Perfect* meant I was performing in every area of my life exactly how I was expected to. I believed the lie that *perfect* meant I was worthy. I was "good enough." I had earned a place in this world. But as it turns out, perfect wasn't possible. It wasn't then, and it still isn't now—not for anyone. Thankfully *grace* is there to set us free from that empty search for perfection. Even if we haven't realized it yet.

Here's the thing about grace: you don't have to be perfect to get it. God's grace is *free*—for imperfect people like you and me. Did you catch that? You don't have to be perfect! I don't either! Jesus took care of that for us. He went before us and made a way. While you're busy planning how to fit in with the popular crowd and get all As on your report cards, God has given us a new standard—a new goal—to reach for. Instead of calling us to be people-pleasing perfectionists, He asks us to "live by following the Spirit," to fill our lives with "love, joy, peace, patience, kindness, goodness, faithfulness, gentleness, [and] self-control" (Galatians 5:16, 22–23 NCV). Nowhere in that list did He mention achieving perfection, sitting with the popular kids, or getting all As.

AS IT TURNS OUT, PERFECT WASN'T POSSIBLE. IT WASN'T THEN, AND IT STILL ISN'T NOW—NOT FOR ANYONE.

In fact, I don't think God really cares a whole lot about any of that. God cares more about us living by His commandments and loving big. He wants to set us free from the traps of perfection and comparing ourselves to others. He's watching us scurry around, saying, "Sweet girls, why are you so hard on yourselves? Why are you so worried and afraid? I've given you all you need."

God is pouring out His grace on us every day, like rain on a thirsty garden. So, if God is giving us so much grace, why on

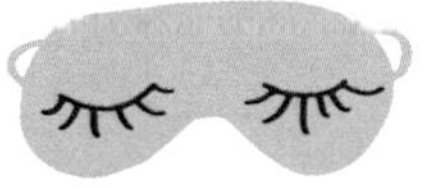

earth aren't we giving a little more grace to ourselves? Why are we running ourselves crazy trying to be perfect? I don't know about you, but it's exhausting. And it's really easy to feel like a hamster on a wheel. We keep running and running, chasing after this idea of perfection and never catching it. Grace, and *only* grace, gives us a way to get off that hamster wheel. This is your time to be young, to mess up and make mistakes, to be silly. Grace is inviting you to take a deep breath, to rest, and to fill your life with the good stuff that truly matters.

IF GOD IS GIVING US SO MUCH GRACE, WHY ON EARTH AREN'T WE GIVING A LITTLE MORE GRACE TO OURSELVES?

Are you stuck on that hamster wheel, trying to be perfect? If so, who defined *perfection* for you? Was it the popular girls, a celebrity, or social media? Was it your mom or someone else you look up to? And does *perfection* really mean living up to someone else's standard? Let's give perfection a new definition, one that gives us some grace and some room to breathe. I'd say giving your best is pretty perfect.

GIVING *your* BEST *is*
PRETTY PERFECT.

## A STANDARD OF GRACE

I don't know about you, but there are days when I feel like I've got this whole "life" thing nailed. And then there are other days when I want to hide in the bathroom with a big bag of gummy bears. For too long I was determined to prove to the world that I could do it all. But here's the thing about doing it all: even if you *can* do it all, no one can do it all *well*.

> HERE'S THE THING ABOUT DOING IT ALL: EVEN IF YOU CAN DO IT ALL, NO ONE CAN DO IT ALL *WELL*.

You are so talented and have so many interests—and I know you want to do it all. Maybe you think you *have* to do it all in order to fit in or to please someone else. So you tell yourself you *can* do it all and do it all really well. How do I know that? Because that's what I did. (And okay, honestly, sometimes that's what I still do.) But it's a lie. And it's a lie that we've let ourselves believe.

I tried to be everything I thought everyone wanted me to be. I tried to be everything for my family, everything for my business, everything for my friends. I honestly believed that being "put together" in every area of my life would equal happiness. Chasing perfection had been my way of searching for joy. But it just didn't work. I wasn't perfect, and I couldn't do it all. There wasn't enough of me to go around. No matter our age, there comes a time when we have to choose what's most important to us. And in order to say yes to what's important, we have to say no—or at least, not right now—to something else. And, sweet girl, that's a good and healthy thing to do.

Let's stop chasing this impossible standard of perfection. Let's hold ourselves to a standard of grace instead.

## MY THOUGHTS

*What does heart-bursting joy look like to you?*

*When was the last time you were heart-bursting happy?*

*How can you add more heart-bursting joy to your life?*

Chapter 2

# WHAT'S IN YOUR WELL?

*Be careful what you think, because*
*your thoughts run your life.*
PROVERBS 4:23 NCV

HOW ARE YOU? LIKE, HOW ARE YOU *REALLY*?

My friend Lara asks me this question a lot. And I can always tell that she's ready for me to lay it all out for her—to tell her how I really am. Isn't it such a gift to spill your heart and be heard by someone who cares? So I'm asking you the same question: How are you *really*? Before you answer, take a minute and take a deep breath. Think about the way your heart is feeling right now, in this minute.

*How are you?*

I'll start. I'm tired just thinking about all the things *you* have to do in your life. As I look around at the girls in my life, I am overwhelmed by how busy you all are. And it's not just in school. You're also active in church, sports, the arts, your communities, and more. You've got family obligations and friendships to juggle. And let's not forget the chores, practices, projects, papers, and tests. You have *a lot* going on.

I know that when I'm feeling crushed by all my responsibilities, I end up doing some not-so-good-for-me things. Like skipping breakfast and staying up way too late trying to get everything done. I don't give myself time to rest, to breathe, to just be still and *be*. I end up running on empty, sputtering like a car down to its last drop of gas. And even though I know better, I feel this pressure to make everyone happy. So I push myself to just keep going. Sound familiar?

One of the biggest challenges we all face is how to give

**YOU** *are a living, breathing vessel of* **GOD'S LOVE.**

ourselves grace in the middle of all the craziness. In my head, I know that means not expecting myself to be perfect. After all, nobody's perfect, right? It also means figuring out how to find some peace and even some joy in this life that's so busy that, let's be honest, some days feel like we're in the circus. But if you're like me, that is a lot easier to say than do. In the end, though, it all comes down to this one fact: being stressed-out and overwhelmed all the time isn't good for you or me—or for anyone around us.

You are a living, breathing vessel of God's love, sweet friend, and so am I. We need loving care, plenty of sleep, good food, and full hearts to be able to grow into the amazing people God made us to be.

Imagine a beautiful car created with attention to every tiny detail. The car is bright and shiny and beautiful on its first trip around the block. But after a while, the car loses some of its shine. It runs to practice and recitals and school. The seats get sticky from spilled drinks. The floors are gritty with crumbs and stale French fries. It splashes through rain, snow, and mud. It gets bumped and scratched and left in a dusty garage. After a while, it's clear the car needs a good wash and vacuum, a refill of gas, and maybe a coat of wax. If it doesn't get some attention soon, that car isn't going to be good for anyone anymore.

Isn't that car just like you? If you run yourself ragged trying to do everything, make everyone happy, and be perfect in every part of your life, you're headed for a crash-and-burn.

## SWEET WATER

Okay, so we're not cars, and we don't run on gasoline. Our hearts are moving, loving, living things. You might say our hearts are like wells—deep and wide. If our well is not being constantly filled up with sweet, fresh water, we are going to run dry. And if our well is poisoned by a steady stream of anxiety, stress, and comparison, then guess what's going to spill out of us? Anxiety, stress, and that feeling that we just don't measure up. Nothing good comes out of a poisoned well.

So how do we get rid of the poison? How do we find that sweet, fresh water? The answer is in Galatians 5:14: "Love your neighbor as you love yourself" (NCV). That line is so powerful. We usually think of it as a command about how to treat others. But it's about *us* too. God is telling us to love, encourage, and take care of ourselves and *then* to love others in the same way. I don't know about you, but if I loved and encouraged my neighbor (or my family or friends) the same way I do myself sometimes, they wouldn't feel very loved at all.

Stop the flow of poison into your heart with a little downtime every day. Step away from the screens that lie and tell you that you aren't good enough. Fill your well with the good

## MY THOUGHTS

*How can I love myself?*

*How can I love others?*

things of life like laughter, true friends, hugs, adventure, and God. That's the kind of sweet, fresh water our lives—and our wells—should overflow with.

You should know that loving yourself isn't anything at all like being obsessed with yourself. And it's not about being vain or full of pride. This is about taking care of yourself—your body, heart, and soul. Because it's only when your well is full that you can truly be who God created you to be. Sometimes that simply means slipping away for a nap or some quiet time with God and His Word. Other times it might mean relaxing with a movie, popcorn, and a best friend. Chances are, you already know what you need to take better care of yourself. The tough part is actually doing it.

Why is it so tough? I think the problem is that we girls—no matter our age or stage of life—want to please everyone. And somewhere, at some time, someone told us that in order to please everyone we had to do it all. We had to earn the grades, make the team, be the star, do the . . . *whatever.* If we didn't, well then, we just weren't quite good enough. So instead of saying yes to only the things that matter to us, we say yes to everything. And we end up without half a second to take a deep breath.

So take half a second. Take a minute. A long minute even.

Breathe in.

Breathe out.

Our world says that being busy is the only way to be. *If we're not going fast*, they say, *then we're not moving*. So we rush and hurry and scurry from one thing to the next. And we set ourselves up for a serious crash-and-burn.

We need to stop and put on our oxygen masks. What does that mean? Well, if you've ever flown in a plane (or watched a movie about flying), you've heard the flight attendants' speech about oxygen masks. It goes something like this: "In the event of an emergency, put your own oxygen mask on first before helping anyone else." Why do they say this? Because if you can't breathe, you can't help yourself or anyone else. The same goes for your daily life. You may be running yourself crazy trying to do everything and make everyone happy, but if you're not taking care of yourself too, you're going to find it hard to breathe.

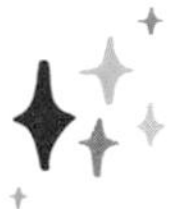

## CRASH-AND-BURN

Let me tell you a story about crashing and burning. Because it's a real thing. And it wasn't that long ago that it happened to me. It was a crazy-busy day. I stood in our driveway, preparing to lift all 150 pounds of our gentle, giant dog into the back of my car. Briggs was a bullmastiff. He was only seven years old, but his legs were already weak. He tried to help by placing his front right paw onto the back bumper of my SUV. I placed my hands under his front left paw and lifted it onto the bumper. Briggs scooted closer to the car while I bear-hugged his back legs and lifted him into the backseat. He turned in circles as best he could in the small space and slowly settled into the car, laying his head on his paws. He was a sweet, sweet pup—an absolute dream of a dog. And he had cancer.

As Briggs's vet appointments became more frequent, I jumped into what I call Captain Mode. I was determined to keep going and get everything done. No matter what. But then that same spring, we lost my father-in-law to cancer. It was a terrible time for our little family. I wrestled with the big questions about heaven and sickness and why bad things happen to good people (and good pups).

> CAPTAIN MODE SAYS, "I'VE GOT THIS. I CAN DO THIS. I CAN MAKE EVERYONE HAPPY. I CAN STEER THE SHIP AND SAVE THE DAY."

Still, I pushed on in Captain Mode. I was going to fix everything. I put all my hope and trust in my own two hands. I skipped meals, lost sleep, and worked harder than ever before. I powered through with the help of caffeine and stubbornness. Does anyone see a crash-and-burn coming? I wish I would have.

One late summer evening I sat on my bed in a mess of tears. I had no peace and no joy. I was afraid of what awful thing would happen next. I sat with my legs crossed and rubbed my hands on my feet with worry. That's when I realized . . . I couldn't feel my foot. The side of my right foot was completely numb.

Of course, I grabbed up my phone and began to Google my symptoms. The internet spat back a whole list of deadly diseases that could explain why my foot was numb. Terrified, I walked around my room, hoping to stomp it out or make it go away. It didn't.

The next morning I made an appointment with my doctor. After telling him about my foot—and all my other symptoms of headaches, eye problems, weight loss, and a racing heart—he ordered a bunch of tests and sent me to another doctor he thought might be able to help me. Weeks later I sat in that doctor's office to hear the news.

"You're perfectly healthy, Emily," he said. "But you are running yourself into the ground. Each of your symptoms is being caused by intense stress on your body. You have to slow down or you're going to make yourself very sick."

I walked to my car in shock. I'd love to tell you that I immediately let go of Captain Mode and that life was wonderful

from that moment on. But I'd put taking care of myself last on my list. I'd stolen the wheel from God, and I'd driven myself straight into a wall. Head on. Crash-and-burn. It was going to take some time to fix this mess.

I hadn't realized that worry, stress, and trying to please everyone could zap the life, energy, and health from our bodies. Since then I've learned to fill my heart and mind and body with goodness: healthy food, water, plenty of sleep, love, joy, God's truth, and moments without stress.

You may be thinking, *I don't want to crash-and-burn. But I don't know how to take better care of myself. How do I fill my life with the good things?* My answer for you is this: Give yourself permission to slow down. Press pause and do a "Life Check." Think about all the things you do. Ask yourself some questions: *What brings me joy? What steals my joy? What's important to me? And what can I say no to?* (And yes, I understand there are some things you *can't* say no to.) We'll talk more about this in a later chapter, but until then, just start thinking about your answers to these questions.

---

**LIFE CHECK:** *What are you missing? What brings you joy? And how can you add more of that to your life, even if it's just a tiny bit?*

---

# I LOVE . . .

I love the beach. I love the way I can see God's creativity in the ocean. I love the freedom of the salty air, the roaring waves, and the sand beneath my feet. I even love how messy I feel at the beach. It's just one of the things that makes me feel *alive*. I also love watching summer sunsets from my front porch. I love having my entire family together. I love laughing with them, telling jokes, and playing games together. I love the white, open spaces at the edges of notebook paper. I love art and creative people and old books and history and fancy dresses. I love stripes, the gospel, guitars, my mama's blueberry pound cake, and the way she takes care of our family. I love long talks with my dad and the way he loves me endlessly. I love writing and singing (though I'm terrible at it). I love country music. I love people.

*I love . . .*

Why, oh why, are we not filling our free time with all these things that we love? Why are we wasting so much time on Instagram? Or YouTube? Or binge-watching another series on Netflix? We could be filling up our wells with so much more of the good stuff. Imagine how much better you would feel if you spent more time doing the things you love.

YOU GET OUT OF THIS LIFE WHAT YOU PUT IN. SO PUT IN SOME JOY.

How much happier would you be if you spent even five minutes a day doing something that brings you joy? Something that makes you feel *alive*? It's not as hard as it might seem to add tiny moments of joy to your life. Wake up twenty minutes early to eat breakfast with your mom and dad. Hang your favorite pictures on your mirror or inside your locker. Stop texting your friends and actually go hang out with them. Love yourself, and fill your life with good things. Remember: you get out of this life what you put in. So put in some joy.

# HOORAY!

*Chapter 3*

# PLAN FOR JOY

*The Lord blesses his people with peace.*

**PSALM 29:11** NCV

WHETHER WE'RE THIRTEEN OR THIRTY-SEVEN, WE'RE all chasing joy. Some joy comes as a surprise, like an unexpected gift from a friend. And some joy comes because you set yourself up for it—you plan for it. In my life, I have learned to make specific choices to create joy.

Personally, I find joy in tidiness. Not just tidiness in my space but also in my time and in my thoughts. Knowing I'm prepared for the week ahead fills me with happiness, peace, and even confidence. So on Sunday evenings, I prepare. Projects are planned. Clothes are laid out. Activities are scheduled. And everyone knows where he or she needs to be and at what time for the whole rest of the week. When all that is done, I feel ready for a good Monday. Of course, that's not possible every Sunday. After all, life is crazy, right? But when it does happen, I feel like I have space to breathe, to enjoy the small stuff, and to spend my week doing more of what I love.

So how do we *tactically* set ourselves up for joy? We start with grace, add a plan, and then end with grace. You might have noticed that my plan for joy includes a double helping of grace. That's because when you make a plan, you need to wrap it up in a giant hug of grace. Why? Because things don't always happen the way you plan. (Again, life is crazy.) Let go of the perfect plan. Create a good and flexible plan—a plan that will give you the freedom to go with the flow, make changes when you need to, and find the joy hidden in the in-between moments.

---

**EVERYDAY CIRCUS:** *The everyday craziness of life*

---

In this chapter, we're going to dive into three systems for taming your own everyday circus: one to organize your time, one to organize your stuff, and one to organize your space. Because creating systems frees up an awful lot of brain space. It brings a little more order, peace, and joy to your everyday circus. And it makes room for the good stuff to happen and for joy to fill up your heart.

# A SYSTEM FOR YOUR TIME: IT STARTS ON SUNDAY

Aren't Sundays wonderful? God gave us Sundays to rest and recharge for the week ahead. For me, that means two things: spending my afternoon preparing for the next six days *and* filling my own tank with the good stuff so I can be the best me I can be. When I designed my Simplified Planner, I included a Weekly Prep checklist on every Sunday space. That's because planning ahead makes a huge difference in setting ourselves up for joy. It makes room in our lives for the stuff that matters most—like actual face time with the friends and family we love.

## *1: Plan for the Week Ahead*

Sunday is the day I sit down and look at all that needs to happen in the next week. And I also think about what I'll need to make that stuff actually happen. For me, that usually involves projects for work and activities with my kids. For you, it's probably things like homework, practices and activities, youth group, and projects.

Sunday afternoons are the time to make sure your homework is caught up. Look at the week ahead—are there bigger projects you need to work on or gather supplies for? Take care of as much as you can.

Sunday is also the day I like to lay out all my clothes for the week. Planning what I will wear on a calm Sunday afternoon avoids that early morning scramble to find something, *anything*, to wear. This is a good time to think about other things you might need during the week too—like cleats for soccer, a glove for softball, sheet music for band practice, a canvas for art class, or shoes for dance class. Gather all those things and keep them in one spot. That way, they'll be easy to grab up as you're on your way out the door.

Just a little preparation on Sunday will make the rest of the week so much smoother. And you'll avoid that scrambled rush to get out the door, forgetting half of what you need.

## LIST-MAKING 101

Lists are my life. Well, not really. But they do make my life so much easier. If you're like me, there are roughly 1,367,489 things swimming around in your brain—dates to remember, things you need to do, papers to get signed, projects to start, and on and on. It's hard to remember them all. That's where lists come in. I take all that stuff that's swimming around in my brain and write it down. Just getting it all down on paper helps me feel less stressed. Here are my best list-making tips:

- Write down everything—no matter how big or small.
- Break bigger things into smaller steps. For example, "Finish science project" could be broken into "conduct experiment," "write report," and "make poster."
- Group together things that are alike. Put all your school stuff in one column and all your chores in another.
- Put the most important, must-do things at the top. Put the "maybe" stuff near the bottom.
- Keep your list where you will see it and remember to check it often.
- Check off each item that you finish—and celebrate, at least a little!

## *2: Tidy Up for a Fresh Start*

I used to think it was so strange that my mom made her bed every morning—and forced us kids to make our own, even when company wasn't coming. *Who's going to see my room?* I thought. *And isn't it just going to get messed up again the next time I go to bed?* I didn't understand her bed-making routine until I had my own house. When my bed is made, I still marvel at how much neater and tidier the whole room seems, even when everything else isn't neat and tidy. A freshly made bed just adds a little bit of peace to my day. Now I understand that Mom wasn't making beds just to keep everything tidy. She was doing it because it felt good to walk into an orderly room. She was setting herself up for peace. And that peace brought her joy.

*The* **WAY YOU BEGIN YOUR DAY SETS** *the* **STAGE** *for the* **REST** *of* **YOUR DAY.**

I follow that same principle in my own house on Sunday afternoons by putting everything back in its place. While you may not have a whole house to keep tidy, you may have noticed that your stuff does seem to wander all over the house. Or at least mine does. Try this quick pick-up trick: Grab a laundry basket and walk from room to room, grabbing anything that belongs to you. Shoes, papers, earrings, cups, laundry, even your trash—it all goes into the basket. (It might take two baskets.) After you've gone through the rest of the house, take the basket back to your room. Toss in anything that's out of place. Next, it's time to sort. Trash goes in the trash, dirty clothes go in the hamper, dirty dishes go to the kitchen—you get the idea. To finish up, put away the things that go in your space, and *voilà*! What could have taken hours upon hours has taken thirty minutes or less.

When you take time to tidy up on Sunday, you can wake up Monday morning to a neat and tidy room. You won't be flooded with tasks: searching for your shoes, digging through dirty clothes for something to wear, or knocking over that stack of dirty dishes on the floor. Instead of running around in a panic to find what you need, your morning will be off to a peaceful start—and who doesn't want that?

The way you begin your day sets the stage for the rest of your day. Here comes the grace hug though: on some days my shoes are left by the couch where I kicked them off, my dirty clothes never make it into the hamper, and my papers are scattered through the house. And you know what? That's okay. Sometimes more important things come up. Maybe it's a friend who needs a shoulder to cry on, a last-minute change in family plans, or a huge homework assignment. The tidying up can wait. But if you can carve out even fifteen minutes to tidy your space, it will make a world of difference.

### SUNDAY TIDY-UP

1. Grab a laundry basket.
2. Gather everything that belongs to you from every room in the house.
3. Gather up everything in your room that is out of place.
4. Sort the stuff in the basket by the room it belongs in.
5. Put it away.
6. Dust off the furniture in your room and clean the floors.
7. Light a candle (with permission). It always makes a room feel fresher.

## *3: Check In and Write Out a Plan for the Week*

Let's face it: we all need a little help getting through the week, no matter how old we are. And because you're young—and probably not driving quite yet—you may need your parents to help you get where you need to go, pick up school supplies or other things for you, or even help you with special laundry and cooking needs. Your parents may also need *your* help with a few things too. Maybe your mom is extra busy one night and needs you to help with a chore or two. Or your dad may need to work late and wants you to take his place in helping a sibling with homework. Checking in as a family and then writing out a plan for everyone's week will go a long way toward cutting back on stress and making everyone's week go more smoothly.

Writing out your plan may sound like a no-brainer coming from someone who owns a planner company. But trust me. I created the Simplified Planner because I get what it feels like to have a million things going on. And I know that you're busy too. There is *so much* to remember. But there is a limit to how much your brain will hold. You need a place to put it all. That's where the planner comes in.

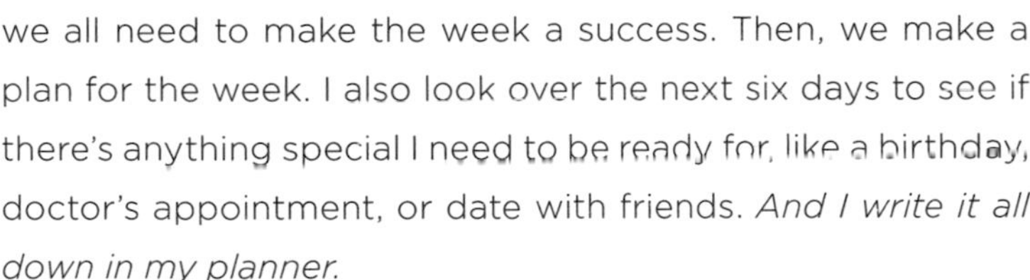

My family and I have developed a routine around writing things out. Every Sunday we check in with each other and compare our schedules for the week. We figure out who needs to be where, when they need to be there, how they will get there, and what we all need to make the week a success. Then, we make a plan for the week. I also look over the next six days to see if there's anything special I need to be ready for, like a birthday, doctor's appointment, or date with friends. *And I write it all down in my planner.*

This sounds like a super-obvious solution, doesn't it? But how many times have you found yourself surprised by something during the week when you knew in the back of your head it was coming? Looking ahead helps you remember everything you need to do. And if you know what's coming in your week, you can help your parents make sure they can get you where you need to be.

Writing out a plan also helps us go with the flow a little better when last-minute changes happen—which is *all the time*. Taking just a few minutes to do this step will save you so much time and stress. And it will also get rid of that nagging feeling that you're forgetting something.

## SUNDAY CHECK-IN

1. Set a weekly tradition to meet with your family to "check in" and compare schedules.
2. Write down any activities and times you need to be somewhere.
3. Think ahead about any special supplies, forms, or equipment you might need. (Do you need construction paper for that science project or a particular book for English class? Does your uniform have a tear that needs mending? Is there a permission slip to be signed for the field trip?)
4. Make notes about any specific clothes or uniforms you might need, especially if you need a parent's help with laundry. (Do you need your uniform for Tuesday's game, practice gear for Thursday, or an outfit for spirit day at school?)

5. Are there any special events or appointments this week? (Do you need a gift for your best friend's birthday, a snack for a class party, or a ride to the dentist's office?)
6. Add reminders for yourself for anything you might need to do some extra preparing for. (Do you have a big project due at the end of the week?)
7. Will you need extra time or help from a parent this week to work on a project, study for a test, or help you rehearse for a play or recital?

## *4: Fill Your Tank*

I'm going to say it again (and again and again, mostly to remind myself): just like a car that has run out of gas, it's hard to help anyone when you're running on empty. You can't be a good friend, a good student, or a good daughter if you don't take care of yourself. Take half an hour after dinner to do something you enjoy. Daydream. Read a good book. Get outside. Hang out with your girlfriends. Soak in God's Word and sing loudly at church. By the time you get to this step, you've probably already tidied your space and prepped for the week ahead. Now, don't forget to take care of yourself too. Take a long shower. Wash your hair. Paint your nails. Do the little things you may not have time for during the week.

I don't know about you, but I feel like a million bucks when my hair is straightened. And when my nails are painted a pretty color, I feel like two million bucks. Feeling just a little more put-together allows me to stand a little taller and tackle the week a little better. That's right: I just told you painted nails are the secret to everything! Of course I'm kidding, but small things do add up. Figure out what those things are for you. Do you feel great after exercising? Give yourself time for a long run on Sunday afternoon. Do you love cooking? Make a really delicious treat to come home to after school this week. Do you love a good book? Read in the bathtub! See what I did there? I paired a feel-good activity (like reading) with a to-do activity (like taking a bath). A two-in-one task, if you will. Those are the best ones to check off because we get to relax *and* get something done.

> YOU CAN'T BE A GOOD FRIEND, A GOOD STUDENT, OR A GOOD DAUGHTER IF YOU DON'T TAKE CARE OF YOURSELF.

## SUNDAY REST

1. Carve out time for yourself in the evening—at least thirty minutes.
2. Turn off the screens and turn on some music that inspires you and settles your soul.
3. Do something you enjoy, just for you. Dive into whatever makes you happiest.

# A SYSTEM FOR YOUR STUFF: CLEARING OUT

Now that you've carved out a system for your time, let's turn to your stuff. Organizing is a *big* job. But it comes with a lot of rewards. Think about the way you feel when your space is tidy. The bathroom is clean. The closet is neat. The laundry is folded and put away. The floor is empty of clutter. The shoes are all matched up and in line. There's something about a tidy atmosphere that *feels* so good. I can tackle the world when my space is in order.

You know why that feeling is so hard to achieve? Two reasons: (1) we're so busy rushing from one thing to the next that we just drop, grab, and run again, and (2) we have too much stuff. Our spaces feel messy and cluttered because there are too many things filling up the space, getting out of place, and requiring our attention. All the stuff steals our focus from what matters—actually living life.

How many times have you rearranged your closet or bought those super-cool, fix-everything organizers to stash all your stuff in? If you have fifty-seven bottles of nail polish, a fancy organizer will make your polish pretty and all in a row, but it's not going to change the fact that you have *fifty-seven bottles of nail polish*! Sometimes the problem isn't our lack of organization; we simply have too much stuff!

**SOMETIMES *the* PROBLEM ISN'T OUR LACK *of* ORGANIZATION; WE SIMPLY HAVE TOO MUCH STUFF!**

There are three types of "stuff":

1. **Stuff we need:** our pillow, the pair of jeans we wear three times a week, and our toothbrush.
2. **Stuff we want to keep:** the award we won, that doll Grandma made, and pictures of family and friends.
3. **Stuff that just takes up space:** last year's science project, T-shirts we don't like, and toys or beauty products we don't want anymore.

We all have these three types of stuff. The question is, what do we do with them? Here's the goal: keep the stuff we need, treasure the stuff we want to keep, and throw away or give away the stuff that is taking up space. We can put a system in place to simplify our space. And a simplified space will free us up to not only get more done but also help us have more peace. Now let's look at how to handle each type of "stuff."

## *1. Stuff We Need*

We all need things like a pillow, shoes, and clothes. But do you really need *all* those T-shirts? How many of those pillows do you actually use? What do you gain from having four different bottles of shampoo? Begin by separating the stuff you need from the stuff you don't.

Grab two trash bags: one for stuff to give away and one for stuff to throw out or recycle. (Beware! You may need more bags!) I like to do one area at a time so that I don't get overwhelmed. For example, you might tackle the closet first. Pull out everything that's trash or to give away and put it into the right bag. Next, you could clean out your desk, bathroom, or space under the bed. (And don't forget about that locker at school!) When a trash bag is full, go ahead and take it to the trash bin. When a donation bag is full, check with your parents about where to take it.

As you decide what to do with each item, remember this: when in doubt, say goodbye. Free yourself from whatever it is and move on. If you have more than one of something—nail clippers, pencil sharpeners, or black T-shirts, for example—choose your favorite one. Toss or donate the rest. You may find yourself with empty drawers or open space in the closet. Don't rush to fill it with something! Allow that space to be empty until you're ready to fill it with something that matters.

## THE BAG PLAN

Mark off each space as you complete it.

- ❍ Closet
- ❍ Desk
- ❍ Nightstand
- ❍ Under the bed
- ❍ Bathroom
- ❍ Other spaces

## *2. Stuff We Want to Keep*

I used to keep a very old recipe tin tucked away in my pantry. Inside it are about sixty handwritten recipes from my grandmother, including her recipe for my favorite blondie bars. She was one of the most special people in my life. Even seeing her handwriting fills my heart with love for the beautiful woman she was and the way she taught me about faith. When I see that little recipe tin, I remember the way she used to hug me tight and say, "You are so sweet, my Emily Sue." It makes me smile even writing that.

One day I decided to move the tin out of my pantry. I put it where there used to be a vase full of fake flowers. Now, every time I walk past that recipe tin, I smile. Want to know how I felt walking past my vase of fake flowers? Blank. Nothing. That tin may not match my décor as nicely as the fake tulips, but it sure fills my heart with something special.

What are the special things in your life? I challenge you to put them where you can see them and smile. For example, gather all those pictures of friends from your phone into a scrapbook or photobook. Keep it on your desk or nightstand. Imagine the happiness you'll experience flipping through them when friends come over. Special treasures belong in special places.

### *3. Stuff That Just Takes Up Space*

You know what this stuff is. You probably stumbled across some when you were figuring out the things you needed to keep. Now, grab your trash bags and go back through your space and look again. Remember, when in doubt, say goodbye. Do you have bins of old toys that you're not going to use again? Give them to your church's nursery, a shelter, or a charity. Imagine how much fun someone else could have with those toys. Are there clothes you know you're never going to wear again? Donate them. If they don't make you feel good when you wear them, toss them out. Make room. Clear some space. Say goodbye. Trust me—the freedom you'll have when you clear clutter from your space is priceless. Empty spaces give you room to breathe.

> EMPTY SPACES GIVE YOU ROOM TO BREATHE.

Figuring out what is trash and what is treasure will keep your stuff from crowding out your life. After all, your things should work for you, not against you. Don't waste time stepping over, dusting, or organizing stuff you don't really want or need. Instead, fill that time with the people and things you love. Those are the treasures that will make your life richer, better, and full of joy.

## MY THOUGHTS

*What are your treasures?*

*Where can you put them so you'll see them often and smile?*

- Empty out the space you're organizing. Seriously, start with a clean slate. Dump the drawer. Empty the locker. Clear out the closet. Put only the necessities back in.

*Master your drop spots. (You know, those stops where you drop stuff and leave it.)*

- Keep only the items you use every day in plain view. Tuck coats, bags, and equipment away in a closet for the next time you'll need them.
- If you keep shoes by your front door, put them in a box or basket.
- Place a shoe box in a convenient spot to drop in keys, permission slips, phones, chargers, and such.

*Create peaceful places.*

- On your nightstand, keep only those items you use before and after you sleep. *Nothing else.* Move all that nail polish to the bathroom. And for sleep's sake, keep your phone somewhere else.
- Create a mini-retreat for yourself in a corner of your room. Add a comfy place to sit, a few pillows, and a snuggly throw. Stack your favorite books nearby. Add whatever you need to make your retreat a true place of inspiration and relaxation. Make your space work for you.
- Replace old art prints and posters with photographs of the people and things you love. Display your special treasures where you can see them often. Remember, this isn't a

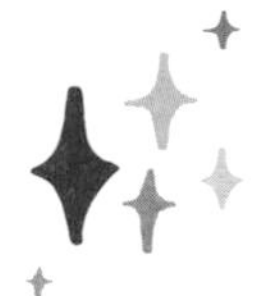

designer room out of a magazine. This is *your* space. Those personal touches that are special and meaningful to you are the best. Being comfortable—not perfectly styled—is the key.

- And don't forget your school locker. Clear out the clutter. Bring in a shelf to help organize the space so you can quickly grab and go. And add something that makes you smile, like a favorite picture, inspirational saying, or Bible verse.

Our physical space has a huge effect on our happiness. The things we fill our spaces with can either inspire us or stress us. By organizing our time, our stuff, and our space, we can make room for happiness and peace. Of course, your happiness doesn't *depend* on everything being clean and tidy. Thinking that way is like hopping a fast train to Anxietyville. Real life can be really messy sometimes. Think of your space as a tool. Use that tool to help you be your best you.

Take a day—like Sunday—to give yourself a fresh start for the days ahead. Choose to say goodbye to the stuff that is just taking up space. Move the things you treasure out where you can see and enjoy them. Donate or toss the stuff that is taking up valuable real estate—both in your space and in your heart. And look for ways to improve the way your space works. Don't overthink this. It's a simple game of yes or no, but it can have a huge effect on your daily life.

SIMPLIFIED

*Chapter 4*

# MAKING MARGIN FOR WHAT MATTERS

*The best memories are often made in the unplanned moments of our lives.*

IF YOU READ THIS CHAPTER'S TITLE, YOU MIGHT BE thinking, *Okay, Emily, but what's margin?* Margin is the white space around the edges of your notebook paper—the space where you don't usually write anything. Leaving that margin empty makes your paper look neater and not so crowded. It's easier to breathe when you're looking at a piece of paper with empty space in the margins. Don't believe me? Try filling up that margin and see how all that crowded space makes you feel.

Just like that sheet of notebook paper, your calendar

should have some margin—some white space—too. It's easier to breathe when there is white space in your life. Yes, there are some things we have to do, like school and church and sleep. These things fill up a lot of spaces on our calendars. But too many of us end up filling all the margins too. And that's when breathing gets a little tougher.

I guess that's because busyness isn't just for grown-ups anymore. If you're like most girls, your calendar probably looks as if an ink pen bled all over it. There's a constant battle for your time and attention. What we spend our time on says a lot about what's important to us. But so many of us have the same calendar problem: when we squeeze activity after activity after activity into our schedules, we squeeze out time for joy. We tell those special moments of joy, "I just don't have time for you. But I sure do have time for extra cheer practice or another violin lesson."

Somewhere along the way, our world decided that we needed the excitement and rush of back-to-back activities and busyness. There's this voice that seems to whisper, *If you don't pack every moment of your life with something to do, you're a loser.* Have you ever heard that voice? Maybe you're trying to rush and go and do so that you feel like you're good enough. (And boy, do I know about that one!) Or maybe you rush and go and do because you're somehow afraid of missing out. You worry that the one thing you say no to will be the one thing that you'll always regret missing. There's even a name for that feeling now: FOMO—the fear of missing out. Sound familiar?

Instead of carefully choosing what we fill our time with, we're caught up in just trying to survive each day. Sure, we *want* to slow down. We *want* to spend more time on the things that matter. But we don't give ourselves permission to do that. Just imagine how many happy moments we're missing out on because we're charging through the day.

## MAX CAPACITY

This may come as a surprise to you: *you have a maximum capacity*. That means there's a limit to how much your body can handle and how much you can stuff inside your brain at one time. If you keep pushing yourself to do more and more, at some point, you'll start to forget things. Assignments fall through the cracks. Chores are forgotten. And it won't take long for you to find yourself in the middle of a giant mess. This is what happens when we're overwhelmed, overbooked, overcommitted, and overstressed.

So what do you do to stop the crazy cycle of busyness? Quit something. Say no. Step away. If your plate is too full, then take some stuff off it.

- Do you go to every movie and party you're invited to—whether you really want to or not? Pick only the ones you really want to attend.

- Are you pushing yourself to go to every afterschool activity and ball game just because everyone else is? Is FOMO causing you to be busy when you'd rather be still? Say no!
- Do you feel like you have to babysit for your neighbors whenever they ask? It's okay to say no.
- Do you really enjoy being on the student council? Or do you serve only because it will look good on your college application? Then don't run for reelection.

It's okay to say no to some things—even good things—so that you can say yes to better things. Of course, there will be some things (like student council) that you won't be able to quit right away. But there are other things you can drop immediately, like mindlessly scrolling through social media or binge-watching another series.

If you're looking for someone to give you permission to slow down—to stop worrying about being perfect and to just be yourself—here it is. You have permission. Don't end up with a numb foot because you won't slow down.

Of course, I understand it's not all up to you right now. Your parents have things they want and need and expect you to do. If you would like to let some of those things go, pick a time to sit down and have a conversation with your parents. That conversation shouldn't include drama or pouting if you don't get your way. If you want your parents to respect what you have to say, you have to do the same for them. Say a prayer beforehand. Ask God to give you words and wisdom. Make a list of why you would like to drop this activity. And make sure it's more than just, "I don't like it." Be ready to answer their questions thoughtfully. Listen when they speak, and accept their answer. If you can't drop a certain activity, ask your parents to help you figure out ways to make it less stressful for you.

You get only one shot at this precious, crazy life. White space in your calendar is priceless. Why work so hard to fill it up? Aren't the in-between moments where we usually find the most joy?

## THE GOOD STUFF OF LIFE

When I was your age, I worried about so many things that turned out not to matter at all. Things like boys and being popular and getting invited to *that* party. And I worried far too much about what others were thinking of me. (I have since learned they were all too busy with their own worries to

---

*Take a look at your calendar. What are the things that stress you out and steal your joy? What can you say no to? What can you take off your plate? Are there conversations you need to have with your parents?*

---

think much about me at all.) There's so much I wish I could go back and tell my younger self. Of course, I can't do that, but I can tell *you*. And maybe you can skip one or two of those hard lessons I learned.

So let's talk about . . .

- Boys—Seriously, there is plenty of time for those guys later. If you haven't already, ask God to lead you to just the right one. And for now, focus on your friends, your relationship with God, and yourself!
- Being popular—Oh, this is a tough one. We all want to fit in, no matter how old we are. But don't let your rush to fit in make you do or say things that aren't true to who you are as God's child.
- Friendships—There are some friendships that last only for a season, and that is okay. Others will last your whole life through—cherish those and take care of them like the precious jewels that they are. (And never, ever neglect your friends for a guy.)
- Mean girls—They are real, and they are called "mean girls" for a reason. Hold your head up and take the high road. Like the Bible says, keep the peace as much as you can (Romans 12:18). And sometimes you'll just need to shake the dust off your feet and move on (Matthew 10:14). Never, ever sink to their level. You're better than that, sweet friend.

The fact is, I once worried so much about pleasing others and fitting in that I missed out on some of the really good stuff of life. Learn from my mistakes. Cherish the good stuff in life *now*. Giggle with your girlfriends. Love on your family. Sing loudly and pray often. You'll never regret it. Yes, there will be some things in life you have to do even if you don't enjoy them. The trash won't take itself out—no matter how old you are. But we waste so much precious time on things that aren't important and don't bring us joy.

These days I try to be grateful for all the little blessings that fill up my days. And I'm less worried about chasing after those big blessings I wish I had. I try to see the joy in *this* moment—the one I'm living right now. Because it's the only one I have right now, and I'll never get another chance to live *this* moment again. I don't know about you, but that makes some of the stuff I fill my days with seem trivial. I mean, who really cares how many likes my photo got?

You don't have to wait until you're all grown up to change the way you think about life. Right this moment you can create a life and a schedule that let you enjoy the good stuff in between all the have-to-dos. You can choose long dinners with your family, game nights with grandparents, and making memories with friends. It can be done. You can find ways to put the good stuff first—instead of letting all the extra stuff take up your time so that there isn't anything left for the good stuff.

Making margin in your day means making room in your

schedule to slow down. It also means choosing to be still even when there are things that you could be doing. It's making sure that people become the most important thing in your day. Yes, the have-tos are still important, but they become less annoying. Going to your brother's baseball game means cheering along with your family. Emptying the dishwasher means gathering clean dishes for a dinner with people you love. Putting away laundry means you are blessed with clothing.

> SOMETIMES THE ONLY WAY TO STEP OFF THE HAMSTER WHEEL IS TO STEP AWAY FROM THE STUFF THAT'S STRESSING YOU OUT.

Choosing to see life in this way will require a big change of heart. For me, that heart change was born out of very tactical steps: taking time to be still, choosing the good over the perfect, and fiercely guarding the pages of my calendar.

## CHOOSING THE GOOD

Here's my best advice—and it's advice I wish I could go back and tell my younger self: don't get so caught up in making everything "perfect" that you miss the good stuff. Because the good stuff is usually hidden in the messy imperfection of everyday life.

## MY THOUGHTS

*What would you do in the margins—the white space—of your days?*

*Where would you be still?*

*Which moments would you savor?*

Our kitchen counters may not be spotless, but the drips of ice cream came from a spur-of-the-moment, late-night sundae party, so I'll happily wipe them up.

My shirt may be wrinkled, but that's because we had a tickle fight on the couch before we left.

I'm not good at baking beautifully decorated cookies for a birthday party. But I'm really good at ordering them from people who are (and that's a talent in and of itself, right?).

"BE STILL, AND KNOW THAT I AM GOD."
—PSALM 46:10

I choose ice cream sundaes, tickle fights, and bakery cookies over stress and perfection. Because those are the good moments that fill me up with heart-bursting joy.

What fills you up with heart-bursting joy? Maybe it's eating cookie dough in sweats and a messy bun while staying up all night with a friend—instead of going to that party where you'll worry the whole time about whether or not your outfit is right. Or perhaps it's spending a few hours digging in the dirt with your dad while he teaches you the best way to plant flowers. It could be hanging out in the kitchen and getting your grandmother to teach you how to make her practically world-famous fudge pie. Or maybe it's simply sitting in the sunshine and soaking up its warmth instead of rushing to yet another extra activity.

Sweet girl, choose the good. Choose the messy. Choose the people you love. Because real life isn't perfect. Sometimes it's a mess. But the mess is worth it.

## A PLANNER WON'T CHANGE YOUR LIFE

You read that right. I'm a "planner maker," and I'm telling you that a planner won't change your life. The fact is, I created the Simplified Planner because I was overwhelmed. I desperately wanted my life to be more simple and structured. But much like a drawer overflowing with fifty-seven bottles of nail polish, my schedule had a clutter issue. I hadn't sorted out what I wanted and what I needed from what was just taking up space.

So I sat down with a big piece of paper and a pen. I decided what I was going to say yes to and what I was going to say no to. First, I gave a loud and enthusiastic yes to my people—my family, my friends—and to the activities and adventures I loved. I said no to my screens and my phone and to all those extra activities that didn't serve me or the people I loved.

Once I figured out what I dearly loved and what I absolutely had to do, I designed a tool to help me keep information written down rather than taking up space in my head. This little tool helped me sort out the have-tos and the want-tos. It helped to carve out margin in my days. And it gave me a peace of mind I'd never felt before.

But the Simplified Planner is not a magic fix. That's because our problem isn't the lack of an awesome planner; it's that we have too many things on our schedules. The magic fix is to strip our schedules down to the things that truly fire us up and to spend our minutes like we spend money: carefully and with plenty of thought. Would you spend your money on the first thing you saw in the store? Probably not, because you want to make sure you get the very best thing for your money. After all, you don't have unlimited cash. And you don't have unlimited time—that's why we have to think carefully about how we spend our days and choose to fill them with the good stuff. We find happiness when we say yes to white space and no to the extra. Happiness happens when we choose the good over the perfect.

## GUARD YOUR CALENDAR

At certain times in life, our calendars are completely full. Maybe you're staying up late to finish a huge project while also juggling sports or band practices. Or maybe there's an illness in your family, and everyone is pitching in to do extra chores. Whatever it is, you're stretched thin, with no relief in sight. Even in those times, I believe that being *intentional* with your time is the key to finding joy. *Intentional* simply means

> WHO SAYS YOU HAVE TO BE SO BUSY ALL THE TIME?

that you think about it. You make a plan. You don't just get swept along with the flow.

As wonderful as you are, there is only so much of you to go around. Every yes you say is a choice; it's a decision to say no to something else. And it's true that sometimes we don't get to choose. There are some things you can't say no to, like homework, church, and chores. But is there a way for you to choose some small yeses to make the burden somewhat lighter? Perhaps you can get together with a friend to study for that big test. Or perhaps you can trade chores with a sibling. Even the tiniest yes can make a big difference.

Say yes to adventure and creativity every chance you get. Say yes to accepting help from friends and family. And say no to feeling guilty for not being perfect and for not being able to do everything. Who says you have to be so busy all the time? Give yourself some grace.

Try this. Make a list of everything that is fighting for your time and attention: school, clubs, sports, chores, practices, church, and youth group activities—everything. Make your list and check it twice. What are the things that aren't really that important to you? What can you give up? Just because you're good at something or just because something is good doesn't mean you have to do it right now. Talk to your parents and ask for their advice. Take ten minutes and figure out what you can quit. It's okay to be a quitter when you're choosing what matters.

## CHECKLIST

Make a list of all the things you have to do. Put a star next to the ones you want to quit. Then talk to your parents about what you can quit and how to do it.

Figure out the things that matter most to you. Then make sure your calendar shows how important those things are. Give yourself the gift of margin.

HAPPINESS HAPPENS
when we CHOOSE the
GOOD over the PERFECT.

*Chapter 5*

# WHEN YOU'RE NOT IN CONTROL

*People can make all kinds of plans, but*
*only the* L*ORD's plan will happen.*

PROVERBS 19:21 NCV

I SAT IN THE CHICK-FIL-A PARKING LOT CHECKING MY email after breakfast. I'd spent the morning catching up with two old friends over Chick-n-Minis. I was nearing five months pregnant with my first child, Brady. I pressed play on a voice mail I'd received earlier that morning.

"Mrs. Ley," said a voice I instantly recognized as my doctor's,

good. But nothing about becoming a mother had gone according to my plans. After months of fear and worry, I gave everything up to God. All I could really do was believe that He was in control.

Weeks later, I lay in the hospital, waiting for Brady to come into the world. I knew then that no matter who Brady was, I already loved him with every bit of my heart. I knew that God had given him to me for a reason. He had prepared me to be his mother. And I was ready.

When Brady was born, the doctor was close to tears herself when she came to my side and said, "Emily, he's beautiful. He's healthy. And he has really long legs."

## TRUST

Brady has been a perfectly healthy, *very tall* little boy his entire life. No one can explain the problems the tests showed. No one except me. Huge things changed in my heart during that time. I was broken down and built together again into a new person. I lost control. And it was in the quiet moments in the middle of the night, when fear overtook me, that God met me. He changed me. And I've never been the same.

Our need to be in control, to create the perfect path for every journey of our lives, causes anxiety to fill our hearts. We try to do and say the right things to get the results we hope for. We don't trust that it will be okay, especially if all the

## MY THOUGHTS

*Which situation are you trying to control right now?*

*Where do you need to let go?*

*What worries are piling up inside you?*

pieces of the puzzle don't fit together the way we plan. And that can lead to comparison, worry, and unhappiness.

What is it for you? Is your life not going as planned? Maybe one of your close friends moved away this year, or all your friends made the softball team, but you didn't. Or maybe you're struggling to believe Psalm 139:13–15, that God made you in an amazing way and that He loves you *just* as you are. Don't spend your months worrying and wishing your life would go as you planned. Don't judge your looks or your home or your life's journey based on some impossible standard. Pray and let go of your worry, trusting that no matter what, God is in control.

> SOMETIMES WE FIND GREATER JOY IN THE MESS THAN IF EVERYTHING HAD GONE ACCORDING TO PLAN.

Sometimes we find greater joy in the mess than if everything had gone according to plan. In my mess, I found quiet moments of togetherness with my husband. I learned what it means to have a faith that cannot be shaken. I learned that family is everything. But more than anything, I learned what it means to let go, to trust God. No amount of hustle, no amount of internet searches, no amount of perfection could bring me ultimate joy. The joy is in the journey with God. Yes, even the hard journeys.

When we're able to let God take control, that's when we find true freedom and true joy.

# GRACE *with* YOURSELF

Your body is a vessel of love, and your heart is a well.
If you neglect yourself, your heart will run dry.
Care for yourself as you would a loved one,
and your heart will overflow with the good stuff of life:
patience, love, kindness, and compassion.

Perfection is overrated.
There is joy in the mess and in the circus
if you allow yourself to be still enough to see it.

Grace is a hand stretched out and
offering to deliver you
from the hamster wheel of trying to do it all.

# Part 2

# GIVE YOUR PEOPLE GRACE

I AM SO GRATEFUL GOD DOESN'T MAKE ME DO THIS crazy life alone. Even though our relationships aren't perfect, how awesome is it that He gives us parents, brothers and sisters, grandparents, aunts and uncles, cousins, friends, and neighbors? Believe it or not, your presence on this earth touches all those people. As perfectly *imperfect* human beings, we're constantly affecting and influencing the people around us. What a huge responsibility!

When we keep that responsibility in mind, it changes the way we treat others. Simple conversations begin to matter more. The morning rush to get breakfast and head out the door becomes just as important as that sit-down dinnertime conversation. The quick text to a friend becomes as important as the heart-to-heart talk at a sleepover. The way you thank the ticket taker at the movie becomes as important as the way you thank someone for a special gift. God's grace shines brightest through us when we love others with patience, gratitude, and acceptance. Never forget that God's not the only one dishing out grace. We have the ability (and responsibility) to give plenty of grace as well.

So why aren't we loving *all* our people—family, friends, and even strangers—like there's no tomorrow? Here's what I've noticed:

- When we feel loved and included, we are more likely to love and include others—good for good.
- When we are thirsty for approval and encouragement, we don't usually use kind or encouraging words with others—bad for bad.

When we're stressed and anxious, we blame the ones we love. And chances are, they will react badly to that, which makes us feel even worse, which causes us to act worse, which leads to . . . you get the picture. It can just keep going on and on in a terrible circle.

What if we chose to pour love on our people and our communities instead? Even when we don't feel like it? I don't know about you, but when I do even the simplest random act of kindness, my heart suddenly feels fuller. And before I know it, I've filled my well up with more of the good stuff—which gives me more to pour out. What a beautiful circle *that* is.

The first step to better relationships and more beautiful experiences with the people we love is simple: *love them.* Love them with a big, unapologetic, awkward, wholehearted love. Love others like God loves you. Fill up your well by filling up someone else's. Say those kind things you sometimes keep inside. Give the hugs. Include others. Let everyone have a seat at the table.

GOD'S GRACE SHINES BRIGHTEST THROUGH US WHEN WE LOVE OTHERS WITH PATIENCE, GRATITUDE, AND ACCEPTANCE.

In this section, we'll talk about what it means to give grace to our families, friends, and communities while also giving grace to ourselves. And we'll explore ways to open our hearts up to God's enormous grace so that we can then pour it out on others. Because there are few things that matter more than giving love and grace to our people.

Chapter 6

# POUR LOVE INTO YOUR FAMILY

*Love never fails.*

1 CORINTHIANS 13:8

YOU PROBABLY DON'T THINK MUCH ABOUT HOW your family interacts. After all, you're with them a good chunk of the week, so it just feels normal. But the people in your family do a lot for you. They provide for you, they help you, they encourage you. They may even be some of your best friends. Each relationship—whether it's with a parent, grandparent, brother, sister, or cousin—affects your thoughts, your time, and your heart. And how you treat your family

Giving grace to your family is hard sometimes. You see each other at your best and at your absolute worst. But when you pour out grace on those closest to you, it creates the kind of relationships that will strengthen you your whole life through.

## GIVE LOVE

It's so important to give love to our families. But how do we do that? What can we do to make sure we're making the most of our time with those we love? Here are some practical things that work for me and my family. Because even though it may not seem like it now, these years of growing up with your family will go by so quickly. You don't want to waste a precious minute.

### *Schedule At-Home Family Nights*

With school, sports, church, and all the activities of life, families today are so often on the go. Times together with everyone at home can be rare. Ask your parents if you can schedule a Family Night each week—even if that night has to change from week to week. Play cards or board games. Pop some popcorn and watch a movie together. Order pizza and have a picnic on the floor. It might sound a bit cheesy, and maybe you think you're too old, but trust me on this. You'll be creating memories that will last a lifetime.

### *Give Each Other Space*

This might sound a bit backward, but it is so important. Sometimes, in order to be closer to the ones we love, we actually need a little time away from each other. My husband, Bryan, needs time away from me and my chatterbox self to unwind and play golf. I need an hour every now and then to watch Netflix or soak in the tub. Time together as a family is important, but it's also good to go your separate ways once in a while. Everyone has different interests, and we all need to be free to explore them. And sometimes we just need to be alone to rest and to think and to be still. Give each other space. Then, when you come back together again, you'll be better able to give each other love.

### *Pick Your Battles*

Don't forget: your sister throwing her stuff all over your side of the room doesn't make her a bad person, so her coat landing on your bed doesn't need to lead to an argument. Pick your battles. Every little thing doesn't need to be hashed out. It's all about showing grace. Let each other be human—and just toss her coat back on her bed.

## BE A MEMORY MAKER

One of the most important things someone ever told me is this: you are responsible for the way you'll look back on your life when you're eighty years old. I know that seems like an impossibly long way off right now. The fact is, though, you're making those memories right now. So think about it. When you're eighty, what do you want to remember about your mom, your dad, your brothers and sisters, your grandparents? Start making those memories now.

- Hang out with your dad. Ask him to teach you his favorite hobby, how to fish, or how to change the oil in the car.
- How about your mom? What's her "thing"? Spend time together, just the two of you. Try to see who she is as a person, not just as your mom.
- Visit your grandparents. Learn that secret family recipe. Listen to the stories. Ask the questions. Find out what life was like when they were your age.
- If you have brothers and sisters, be their biggest encouragers. Make the signs, lead the cheers, and be a part of their lives.

You don't need a holiday, a big event, or a special day. The most precious memories all have one thing in common: time spent together. So spend some time—and make some memories—with the ones you love.

## MY THOUGHTS

*What traditions does your family have?*

*What traditions would you like to start?*

Chapter 7

# ENJOY THE CIRCUS

*Life can be like a three-ring circus. The secret to being happy is learning to enjoy the show.*

A THREE-RING CIRCUS IS A CIRCUS WHERE SHOWS are happening in three different rings, all at the same time. Or, according to the dictionary, it can also be "something wild, confusing, . . . or entertaining."[1]

I think *three-ring circus* is a good way to describe life. It can certainly be wild, confusing, and entertaining.

Look at your own schedule. Are you living a circus? How often do you juggle school, homework, chores, practice time, friend time, family time, and God time? All in the same day? No matter how great your juggling skills are, there's always

*Chapter 8*

# GIVE GRACE TO YOUR COMMUNITY

*Sometimes the best way to make friends is second-grade style.*

IT'S EASY TO FEEL ALONE WHEN YOU'RE IN THE THICK OF it, to feel like no one else in the world understands the battles you fight or the life you live. But this idea—that no one else can possibly understand—keeps us from connecting with others. The truth is, we're all dealing with a lot of the same worries and fears, especially when it comes to making friends. We're worried we'll be rejected if we reach out to someone. Or we're afraid of how hard we'll have to try to make friends. Sometimes it feels easier to be alone and to stick to what we know.

and kind, and they truly want the best for each other. They're the people you're safe with. They don't take your heart's secrets and hold them up for the world to see. They encourage and build up. They don't shame or tear down.

But you and I know that not all "friends" are true friends. That's why we need to offer kindness to everyone, but we need to be very careful who we share our hearts with. Frenemies are a real thing. They're the people who pretend to be your friend but are quick to betray you when it suits them. And then there are the mean girls who don't even bother pretending to be a friend. Take the high road. Don't return their evil with more evil. Because even if you win, you lose—and you don't really want to be like them, do you?

## CREATING A COMMUNITY OF FRIENDS

Sometimes the best way to make friends is second-grade style. Just say hi—yes, even to girls you don't know. Think up reasons to get together (and get to know each other). Do you both have the same big test coming up? Study together. Are you both superhero fans? Invite her to see the next big movie together. We can't just sit around and wait for a new friend to find us. We have to put ourselves out there and seek friendship.

aren't we all just girls trying to do life well—cupcakes, perfect nails, or not?

Now, let's think about the kind of community we don't want to have. Start by asking yourself, *Why do I follow people who make me feel less than good about myself?* Now, here's my advice: unfollow anyone who makes you feel "less than" who God created you to be.

Does someone else's constant bragging make you feel like you're not keeping up? *Unfollow.* Does someone's snarky comments about others make you feel uncomfortable? *Unfollow.* Do you follow some people from school just to make sure you're not missing out on the best gossip? *Unfollow.* Do you follow someone so that you can feel like you're better than she is? *Unfollow.* Are there people on your friend list that you're not sure why you followed in the first place? *Unfollow.*

That unfollow button is there for a reason. Don't let social media hurt your heart with a thousand tiny pinpricks. Make your online world a place of inspiration, genuine friendships, and joy. Guard your heart, because what you put in it is what you'll hand out to everyone around you. (While you're at it,

---

**UNFOLLOW FRIDAY:** *Every Friday, join me in picking one person or thing to unfollow online. Make your online world a place of inspiration, genuine friendships, and joy.*

---

make sure *you're* not doing or saying anything on social media that could hurt or cause others to feel "less than.")

Community is everything, so build it carefully and thoughtfully.

## THE PEOPLE IN YOUR NEIGHBORHOOD

While we're on the topic of building community, it's so important to notice the other people in our communities. Maybe it's the server at our favorite restaurant, the receptionist at school, or the school bus driver. How can we give grace and love to those people? By going out of our way to be kind and thoughtful.

When I was seven, I attended the same elementary school where my mom taught fourth grade. At the end of every day, I did my homework in my mom's classroom until she finished her work. One afternoon my mom overheard two female custodians talking in the hallway. For the first time ever, one of the ladies wouldn't be hosting Thanksgiving dinner because she couldn't afford a turkey. Mom told me what she had heard. Brokenhearted, I asked what we could do to help. So we pooled what was in her wallet and the coins from my piggy bank and headed to the grocery store. We had just enough money to buy the biggest frozen turkey available. Little baggie of money in hand, I trailed behind my mom as she placed the frozen turkey at the register. I counted out the coins and dollar bills and paid for the turkey.

The next morning we quietly gave our friend the turkey. She was endlessly thankful. But the real gift wasn't in what she said or did. The real gift was to a little girl named Emily, who learned how random acts of kindness can spread love like wildfire.

My mom taught me that one of the best ways to build a community and spread love is to look for needs and find ways to meet them—not just with our money but with our friendship as well. Be an includer. Look for people who are alone and bring them into the group. It's the small, quiet acts of love that can show God's love in deeply meaningful ways. By using what you have, right where you are, you can send waves of grace through your community—just like little Emily and her piggy bank of coins.

Two people are better than one, because they get more done by working together. If one falls down, the other can help him up. But it is bad for the person who is alone and falls, because no one is there to help. If two lie down together, they will be warm, but a person alone will not be warm. An enemy might defeat one person, but two people together can defend themselves; a rope that is woven of three strings is hard to break.

**—ECCLESIASTES 4:9–12 NCV**

*Chapter 9*

# IT'S ALL ROUTINE

*There is a time for everything.*

ECCLESIASTES 3:1 NCV

ROUTINES, TRADITIONS, AND HABITS—THEY CAN TAKE an otherwise mess of a day and make it more peaceful. Knowing what's going to happen next and that there's a plan to make sure everything is taken care of gives us a feeling of safety and security.

But order and organization don't happen by accident. Most ordinary human beings don't jump out of bed every morning ready to be a blessing to the world. No, these things happen when we set ourselves up for success and when we remove a bit of chaos to make space for grace. Think of a time when you felt ready to take on the world because all your homework and chores were finished. Chances are, you made wise choices with your free time in order to get to that finish line.

So how do you take control of your days rather than letting your days control you? Routines! Once you trim your schedule down to the things that truly matter, you can create routines for making sure those things happen. Then you're left with the precious gift of margin—time to spend filling yourself up with the good things of life. Good things like taking care of yourself and loving on your people.

Routines and systems make my life run smoothly. Every day there are certain chores and activities that have to be done. So I create routines and systems to get them done. And while everything doesn't always happen exactly the way I plan, routines make me feel a little more relaxed and a lot less frazzled. But before we dive into the routines that work best in my life, let me say this in giant letters: BE FLEXIBLE and GIVE YOURSELF SOME GRACE.

Some days will go perfectly according to plan. Other days will not. You'll spill orange juice on your new white shirt right as you're about to rush out the door. The dog really will eat your homework. Or that science project you just knew was due next week is actually due tomorrow. So be flexible. You might not get all your clothes ready for the next day because practice ran late. That's okay. Give yourself plenty of grace.

To pin down your best routines, start by figuring out

**BE FLEXIBLE *and* GIVE YOURSELF *some* GRACE.**

## MAKE YOUR MORNINGS EASIER

- DAILY TO-DOS: At the end of every day, write out your to-do list for the next day. Putting it all on paper will help you clear your brain for the evening and rest better.
- WRITE DOWN YOUR DAILY ROUTINES: Write down every little task that clutters your morning and see if you can do some of them the night before.

## THE RULES OF BALANCE

Have you ever heard the term *balancing act*? It's a term people use when they talk about trying to create a perfect balance between work and family and friends. But honestly, I don't think it's possible to create a perfect balance. Instead, I think God pulls us back and forth, from work to family to friends. There will be days when work—like school or chores or projects—needs more attention. Then there will be other days when family or friends need us more. We just have to go with the flow. It's like riding a bike: we're never really perfectly balanced. We're constantly shifting our weight from side to side to keep from face-planting.

Here's the thing: I love my work. And I adore my family and friends. To make sure I keep my attention where it's needed most, I have a list of rules that help me make sure the things that matter most to me get the best of my attention.

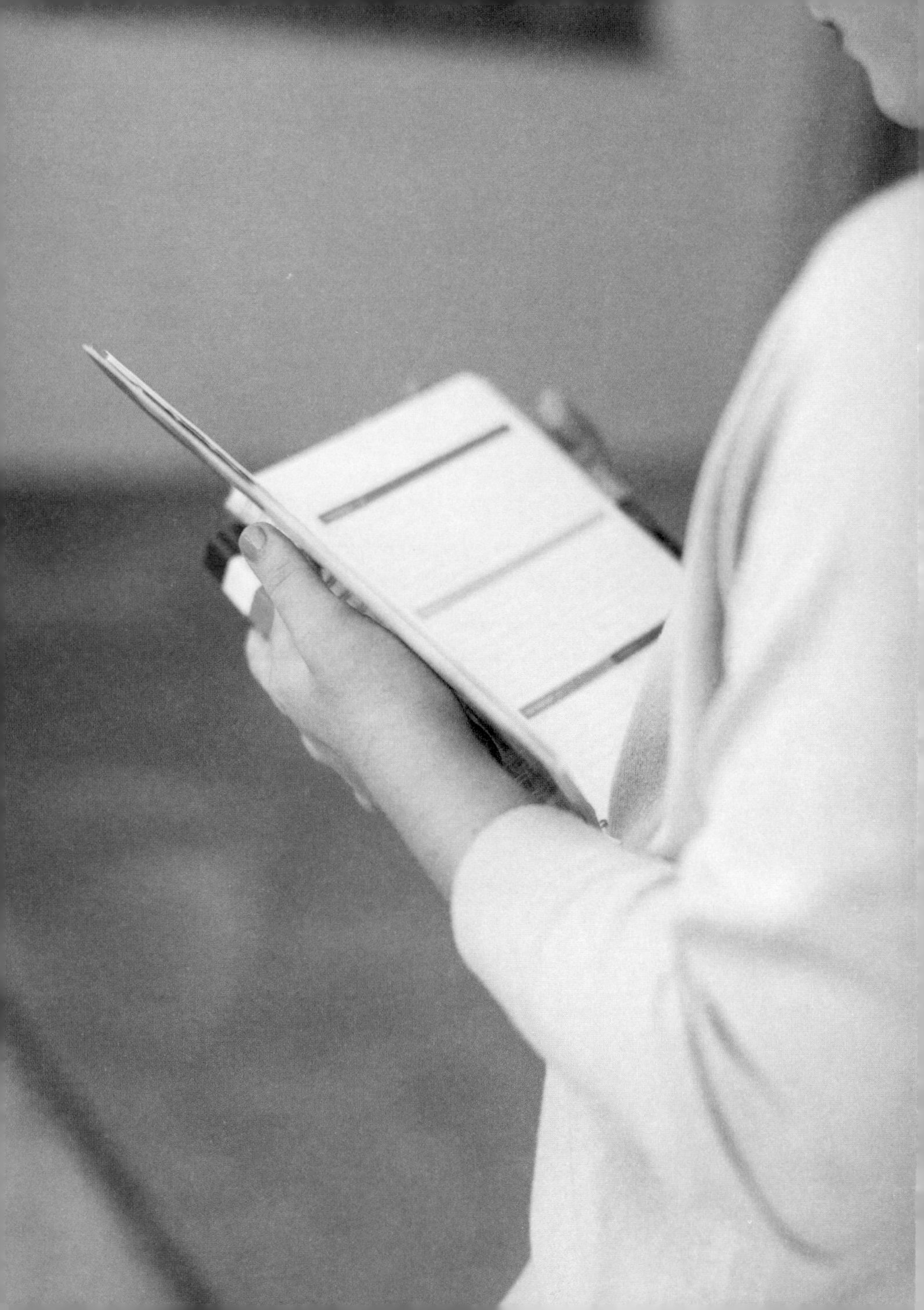

- Make it a competition. How fast can you unload the dishwasher? Can you beat your best time?
- Use your imagination. Set a timer and race to save the world by detonating the bomb (also known as taking out the trash) before the timer rings. Or put on your favorite pump-up music and try to finish before the song ends.

Routines create peace. There's a feeling of security that comes with knowing what comes next. Though your plans may change, it's certainly nice to know there's a plan in place. I don't stress about what to wear in the morning, because I've laid my clothes out the night before. I know I'm going to have clean hair because I wash it in the evenings. Those plans make a real difference in how I approach my day. They get rid of a lot of the stress.

My dad always says, "If you fail to plan, you plan to fail." Just a few minutes of planning can take away hours of stress and worry. And it will give you the peace you need in order to give more grace to your people.

## Chapter 10

# A GRATEFUL HEART CHANGES EVERYTHING

*Do not worry about anything, but*
*pray and ask God for everything*
*you need, always giving thanks.*
PHILIPPIANS 4:6 NCV

MY DAD IS MY HERO. HE'S STRONG AND KIND. HE could probably build an entire house by hand if you asked him to. He's the most giving man I've ever known. And he's just plain smart. He can turn a comment about romaine lettuce into a discussion on the iguanas of Tahiti. Before you know it, he's rattled off seven different kinds and their Latin names. The man's an encyclopedia. He's the one I call when I'm worried or have questions about, well, anything. Basically, I hit the dad jackpot.

My dad loves fishing. For years, he dreamed of owning his own boat. He finally bought one when I was a teenager. He and my younger brother, Brett, took the boat out for the first time one early Florida morning before dawn. My mom and I couldn't wait to hear how their day on the water had gone. Just a few hours later, though, my mom rushed into my room with a phone in one hand and her keys in the other.

"There's been an accident," she blurted. "Get in the car."

My dad and brother had been having the time of their lives until my dad's line got stuck on a buoy. When he yanked the line back to unhook it, it snapped and hit his eye. After multiple surgeries, he was left blind in his left eye.

My little brother and I learned so much from the way our dad handled that experience. We saw him dig up all the courage and gratitude he could find to get through one of the most difficult experiences of his life. Day after difficult day, he talked about how grateful he was to have been born with better-than-perfect vision in both eyes. Even with the loss of his left eye, his right eye was able to do the job. He also told everyone how proud he was of my brother for driving the boat to the dock so he could get to the hospital quickly. Dad always chooses to see the good in every situation. Instead of focusing on the loss of sight in his eye, he chose to be amazed by the ways God provided for him.

## CHOOSE WHAT YOU SEE

*Perspective* is a big word that simply means how you choose to look at things. And perspective is everything. Like with my dad. He could have focused all his thoughts on losing sight in one of his eyes. But he didn't. Instead, he chose to look for the blessings.

Perspective is kind of like using a camera lens—and God lets us operate the camera. We get to choose what we zoom in and focus on. If we focus on all that is wrong, we'll end up with a grouchy, sour attitude. But if we focus on what is good and right, we'll end up with a grateful attitude. And our attitude will rub off on the people around us. Younger kids will learn from the ways we handle the ups and downs of life. Our friends will be either discouraged by our constant complaining or encouraged by our constant thankfulness. We can choose to think about everything that's gone wrong and our mistakes and the mistakes of others. Or we can choose to focus on all that God has blessed us with—the big and obvious things as well as the tiny, hidden pieces of goodness.

Yes, God may have you walking through a terrible time in your own life, but the camera is yours. You control what you focus on—even when you can't control the situation. Choose to be grateful. Choose to focus on the blessings and goodness. And choose to give grace—to yourself, to the situation, and to others. Because grace and a grateful heart go hand in hand.

**GRACE** *and a*
**GRATEFUL**
**HEART** *go*
**HAND** *in* **HAND.**

## CHANGE YOUR FOCUS

When I find myself feeling overwhelmed or sad, I try to change the focus of my "camera" by listing what I'm grateful for. I even started a gallery wall in my house to help me do this. I've filled with it pictures of answered prayers. There's a photo from our wedding day, each of our children's first photos, a hand drawing of our house, and pictures of our parents, grandparents, and all the rest of our families. Just one peek at that wall puts my heart in the right place. Remembering all I have to be grateful for helps pull me out of whatever pit my heart might be stuck in.

So often I shove my gratefulness down into a hole and tell it to stay there. Why? For silly reasons! Because my house

---

♥ *What are you grateful for? Make a list. Big things and small things. It can be everyday things and once-in-a-lifetime things. It might be family and friends. Or it might be people, pets, and places. What are the blessings in your life?*

- ____________________
- ____________________
- ____________________
- ____________________

or the funny in any situation. Here's just one example: When my dad returned to work after losing sight in his eye, he set a little stuffed Mike Wazowski on his desk. Mike is the silly one-eyed monster from Disney's *Monsters, Inc*. I'm guessing that some of Dad's coworkers may have been uncomfortable going into his office for the first time after his accident, but they were soon doubled over in laughter. My dad refused to let the accident take away one of his most precious gifts: his sense of humor.

Dad's ability to find joy after such a tragedy taught me that God gives grace in so many ways. He gives us humor when it's hard to laugh. He gives us a new perspective when life feels so hard. And He gives us friends to help us get through the highs and lows of life with joy. What incredible gifts from our incredible God!

---

♥ Take a minute to write down three situations you're facing right now that seem hopeless. Is there even a tiny nugget of hidden silliness anywhere in them? Is there something to be grateful for that could help you see the blessings even in this situation?

________________________________________

________________________________________

________________________________________

What things bring you the most joy? The deep, uncontrollable, belly-laugh kind of joy? Make a list below.

## GRATEFUL GRACE

Yes, humor and gratitude are wonderful for getting us through our everyday messes. And yes, they turn things around for us by helping us focus on our blessings. But what about when you're stuck in a hopeless situation? When no amount of positive thinking can cover up the hurt? Whether it's an illness, your parents' divorce, or the death of someone we love, God meets us with grace in those spaces too. When everything is out of our control, that's when God steps in and shows us just how good His goodness can be—and just how good His people can be.

When I was a little girl, my grandmother lost her car while shopping at a department store. She walked the aisles of the parking lot until security noticed her panicked look and helped her find it. It was the beginning of Alzheimer's, a heartbreaking disease that robs people of their ability to think and remember. My mom watched as her mother suffered from this disease. And I watched as my grandmother, who we called Grandmommy, forgot my mom's name.

The time came when Grandmommy had to go to a nursing home. From that point on, my mom went to visit Grandmommy every single day. And I went with my mom many times—wearing my prom dress, my graduation cap and gown, and eventually my wedding gown. My mom never wanted her mom to miss out on a thing, even if she couldn't attend those events herself. My mom kept the candy bowl full in Grandmommy's room (for all the nurses, of course) and had a bag of makeup and hairspray handy to get Grandmommy ready for the day.

> WHEN WE SHOW GOD'S LOVE AND GRACE, WE ARE LIVING, BREATHING EXAMPLES OF HIS PERFECT LOVE.

You see, Grandmommy had always been a glamorous lady. Every Friday of her adult life she'd gone to "the beauty shop" to have her hair done. She took me to fancy restaurants when I was little and taught me ladylike table manners while I wore white gloves. She was a woman of class like no other. And even as my grandmother's memory faded, my mom did what she could—she made Grandmommy beautiful every single day. Talk about showing up and giving grace to your special people, even when it's hard!

I learned a lot from watching my mom serve and love her own mom. I learned that God will fill your cup and give you the strength to do what you need to do. He does it so we can serve and love our people. When we show God's love and grace, we are living, breathing examples of His perfect love.

God desperately wants us to spread His big, bold love all over the place. And He meets us in the middle of our crazy days to help us do just that.

---

♥ Is there someone in your life who you can really show up for with grateful grace, just as my mom showed up for my grandmother? Maybe an elder in your church is sick, and you make him or her a meal. Or maybe your sister sprained her ankle, and you volunteer to take on her chores for a while. Take a moment to think about your friends, family, and community, and write up some ways you can share God's grace.

*Part 3*

# THE GRACE TO BE YOU

WHAT WERE YOU PUT ON THIS EARTH TO DO? OR maybe the better question is this: *Who* were you put on this earth to be? God has given you a *calling*—something He created you to do. He wrote it on your heart when He made you. It can take some time to discover exactly what that calling is, so don't worry if you don't have it figured out yet. (In fact, a person's calling can change over the course of her life.) I believe God has lit a tiny flame inside you that's just waiting to be discovered and fanned into a roaring fire. But how do you do that? How do you find and then do the job He's asked you to do?

In Luke we're told that, "Where your treasure is, there your heart will be also" (12:34). Whatever you can write, sing, or talk about for hours—that is the calling God's leading you to. You were created to do a very specific and very important job in God's kingdom. Sometimes your calling is right in the middle of your everyday life. Other times it's a neon-bright blinking star guiding your steps as you go. Whatever your calling is, when you find it, chase after it with your whole heart. Dive into it fully. You were made to be great.

In these next few chapters, we're going to talk about what it means to chase after your calling while still giving yourself plenty of grace. We'll talk about ways to trust the journey you're on and how to pick yourself up gracefully when you fall down.

*Chapter 11*

# THE LIFE YOU WANT TO LIVE

*"I know what I am planning for you," says the Lord. "I have good plans for you, not plans to hurt you. I will give you hope and a good future."*

**JEREMIAH 29:11** NCV

**I REMEMBER WHAT IT WAS LIKE TO BE YOUR AGE. YOU'RE** not a small child anymore, but you're not quite a grown up either. It's a time when anything could happen. As you're looking at the next few years ahead, it probably feels like there are a hundred different roads you could choose to follow. It's both a beautiful and terrifying place to be. People are starting to ask you questions like, "What do you want to be when you grow up?" And maybe some of your friends seem to have it all figured out. Some of mine certainly did. But I had absolutely no idea what I wanted to do with my life. All I knew was that I wanted the chance to be creative. I wanted to inspire people. I wanted to be challenged and pushed in my work, and I wanted a family of my own. Basically, I wanted it all—but I wasn't quite sure how to get there. None of the roads looked like the one I felt God was paving in my heart. None felt right for me. I hit my knees more times than I can count and asked God to tell me what I was supposed to be when I grew up. Finally, I decided to look for my treasure—my calling: "For where your treasure is, there your heart will be also" (Luke 12:34).

I didn't know where I'd end up or who I'd become, but I knew I loved books. I loved Emily Dickinson and Ernest Hemingway and Mark Twain. I was the little girl who hid beneath her covers with a flashlight, reading into the wee hours. I loved the way words could paint a story and the way a paragraph could move my soul to feel and experience the wonders of this glorious life. I loved the way writing freed my heart and helped me make sense of the world around me.

I really believe that God lit a fire in me for writing *because* He wanted me to follow the path of my passions. So what if those passions didn't lead to a clear-cut career like being a doctor, a pilot, or a teacher? Instead of choosing a clear path for the rest of my life, I chose the uncertain path of following my passions. And it was one of the best decisions I've ever made.

I am blessed with parents who told me they were proud of me. They encouraged me to follow my heart and my dreams. They told me I could join the circus if I really wanted to. My parents gave me permission to follow my passion and to run full speed ahead down the path my heart was burning for. That changed my life, and I am so grateful for them and their encouragement. No, it hasn't been a perfect path. But it has been messy, fun, wild, and free—and mine. I tell my son Brady every day that if he really wants to be a cupcake maker when he grows up, I'll be first in line to try every new flavor. I'll even stand outside and wave a big cupcake sign at the cars driving by.

> IT HASN'T BEEN A PERFECT PATH. BUT IT HAS BEEN MESSY, FUN, WILD, AND FREE.

Maybe this is all unfamiliar to you. Maybe no one ever looked you in the eye and gave you permission to follow your wildly unique, custom-made heart. Let me promise you this: God is the ultimate parent. And as much as I want my boy to follow his dreams, God wants that even more for you. So let me say to you what I'd say to my kid:

> Sweet precious one, if you are ever worried about what God is calling you to do with your life, listen to that heart of yours. Run like crazy down the path God has set your

heart on fire for. The God who loves you will be around every corner, cheering you on. Be yourself, sweet one. Trust that heart God so tenderly gave you. If you don't know what your calling is yet, that's okay. Keep trying things until it finds you. And in the meantime, you *can* build a life you dream of.

## BUILD A LIFE

Whether it's youth group or clubs, activities or sports, what you *do* is just one tiny part of your life. But there's so much focus on it, right? Will you go out for this team or be a part of this club? Will you take this class or go on that retreat? What if you focused less on choosing clubs, activities, and groups—the things you do? What if you focused on choosing a *life* instead? Whether you're twelve, twenty-seven, or seventy-seven, you can begin to build the kind of life you want to have. And this stage of life you're in is the perfect time to begin deciding how you want to spend your days. Every single day is a gift from God. What if you chose to live each one to its absolute fullest?

EVERY SINGLE DAY IS A GIFT FROM GOD. WHAT IF YOU CHOSE TO LIVE EACH ONE TO ITS ABSOLUTE FULLEST?

Don't just shape your life around what you do. Shape what you do around the kind of life you want to live. Who says you have to spend every minute rushing from school to practice to homework to bed—only to get up and start it all over again the next morning? You, my friend, have options. Yes, it's true there are some things you have to do. And because you are still learning and growing, there are some things your parents expect you to do. But you can create a life around those "have to dos" that is beautiful and meaningful to you.

Remember, you're just starting out in this whole life thing. Explore. Dare to try new things. Risk messing up. Don't be afraid to fail. Failing is really just learning what's not right for you. It will take some hard work and some planning. It will take conversations with your parents. But it is possible to create the life you dream of—both the life you're living right now and the life you want in the future.

*What words would you use to describe the life you dream of having?*

I've made every mistake you could ever imagine. And I've fallen on my face more times than I can count. But through it all, God has shown me that even though the path of life is full of rocks and mud and muck, the flowers blooming along the path are too beautiful to miss. He's given me strength and courage and patched up my skinned knees more times than I can count.

WHAT SETS YOUR HEART ON FIRE? WHAT STORY IS GOD WRITING WITH YOUR LIFE?

So here are my questions for you: What sets your heart on fire? What story is God writing with your life?

The fact is, your life is going to be changing a lot over the next few years. You're heading for high school, possibly college, and then a life beyond. You're going to need to be ready to roll with those changes. Don't let them roll over you and flatten you. Right now is the time to figure out who you are, deep down in your heart and soul. Who and what do you love? What matters most to you? What makes you *you*? Hold tight to these truths about yourself through all the changes of these coming years. God is using you in a very specific and special way. Let Him lead you. Give in to His gentle tug—and He will change your life and give you one that's even greater than your dreams.

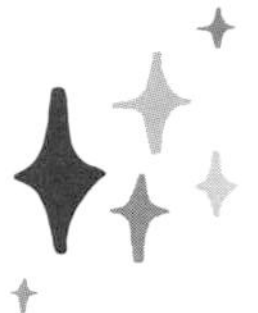

## FOLLOW THE TUG

To figure out where your heart is leading, you need to spend some time figuring out who you are. For me, this happens with a pen and paper. I love a good Sharpie and a big plain white piece of poster board. There's something about pouring out my heart and mind onto a blank page that makes everything clearer. Try it for yourself: Grab that Sharpie and poster board. Spread out on the floor. And just start writing down all the things you love to spend your days doing. Don't worry about being neat or putting everything in a row. Draw arrows and stars. Write big and small. Pour out your heart. Then study your words. Do you see any patterns? Are there any themes that keep popping up, like reading books, loving God, being outdoors, playing sports, or serving others?

Use your words to paint a picture in your mind of the life you want to have. Think about the big and the small—from how you'll spend your time after school hours to what your future career could be to what you want your everyday routines to look like. This exercise is great to do every few months as your life and your interests change.

What are your must-haves in life? What experiences, adventures, and little life luxuries do you want? For me, I

## HEART'S CALLING WORDS

Do any of these words fit your heart's calling?

writing
crafting
organizing
photographing
designing
building
cooking
storytelling
volunteering
performing
loving
helping
traveling
creating
leading
giving
drawing
painting
encouraging
planning
reading
noticing
recording
dreaming

want to be free to spend Fridays with my kiddos. Sometimes that means I have to work late the other days of the week. Perhaps you want to have Saturday mornings free to paint or write or spend time with friends. What might you need to sacrifice to make that happen?

You may not be able to make all of your must-haves work. At least not right now. But don't let that stop you from imagining the life you want for yourself. What steps can you take now to put you on the path to the life you want to have? Building the life you want isn't easy, but it is so, so worth it.

WHAT ARE YOUR MUST-HAVES IN LIFE? WHAT EXPERIENCES, ADVENTURES, AND LITTLE LIFE LUXURIES DO YOU WANT?

---

♥ Describe the life you want to build for yourself. Don't worry if it's out of your reach right now. It's only after naming your dream that you can try to make it happen. Revisit your dreams every few weeks or months. What has changed? What has stayed the same?

*Chapter 12*

# DON'T BE AFRAID OF GETTING DIRTY

*"When people fall down, don't they get up again? And when someone goes the wrong way, doesn't he turn back?"*
**JEREMIAH 8:4 NCV**

WHEN YOU OWN YOUR OWN BUSINESS LIKE I DO, AT some point, you wear all the hats. Not only will you be the big boss CEO, but you'll also be the assistant, the advertising department, and the cleaning crew. Sometimes all at once. But when I first started my business, I didn't want anyone to know I was doing it all. So I set up lots of email addresses like Accounting@EmilyLey.com or PublicRelations@EmilyLey.com. I spent tons of money on business cards. I wanted to build the perfect "real business" image so everyone would instantly think I had it all figured out. Even though there was just me, I used words like *we* and *us* and *our* to keep up the big-company image. I even used all the money I made during the first two years to pay for an incredibly trendy website. It was gorgeous. Lots of burlap and white and vintage stamps. It definitely was not my preppy happy-stripes-forever style, but it was totally gorgeous. I did it because that was the style the rest of the world seemed to be using at the time.

I simply wasn't proud to have a teeny-tiny company. I worried that customers would choose bigger brands because they couldn't trust a one-woman show. If I was going to be in business, I thought, I needed to be big right out of the gate. Oh, if I could only tell that younger me what I know now.

One week before my brand-new website launched, I got an email. A punch-you-in-the-stomach kind of email. It was from a lawyer telling me that my business name (which was not Emily Ley at the time) was trademarked. I would need to change it immediately. I stared at all those expensive new business cards and that fancy website and realized I'd made a terrible mistake.

God used that giant bump in the road to direct me toward the real mission He had for me. I changed my company name to my own name. I redesigned my brand and website and business cards. I gave up on trying to make everyone think

## Chapter 13

# THE LIES ARE EVERYWHERE

*"The truth will set you free."*

**JOHN 8:32**

**T*HE LIES*. THEY'RE LIKE A PLAGUE. THEY'RE EVERY**where, and they are so deadly to our hearts. They tell us things like, *You just being you is not good enough*. Or, *You aren't special or important*. Or, *You're just too much—too much effort, too much trouble*.

Here's the thing about so many of the lies: they come from comparing ourselves to others. It might be people we know, celebrities, or posts on social media. And every time we listen to the lies, they get bigger and louder and easier to believe.

## FIND THE TRUTH

How do we get rid of the lies? How do we free ourselves from the trap of believing we're not enough? *We find the truth and believe it instead.* After years of battling so many of the same lies you battle, I can tell you that God absolutely does not want us to believe them. Instead, He wants to fill our lives with these beautiful truths:

1. You are not only good enough, you are God's own wonderfully and fearfully made creation. (Psalm 139:14)
2. You are special and so important that God has created a plan for your life. (Jeremiah 29:11)
3. And you are never too much—too much effort or too much trouble—because God loves you so much that He sent His only Son to save you. (John 3:16)

Sweet girl, I'm stomping my feet and shouting this at the top of my lungs so you can hear it from sunny Florida: *You are fearfully and wonderfully made. YOU ARE ENOUGH.*

Please stop worrying about whether you're wearing the right clothes or fitting in with the right crowd. And please stop wondering if you are too much or just not enough. In fact, here's a handy quiz to help you see how wonderful you really are:

1. Are you kind, helpful, and encouraging?
2. Do you try to love and serve others?
3. Are you trying to be the best friend, daughter, or sister you can be?
4. Are you trying to live the way God wants you to live?

Then you are fabulous! You're doing it, friend! Tell the lies to get lost. Ain't nobody got time for that nonsense.

Notice that I didn't say you were doing any of those things perfectly. Believing you have to be perfect is just another lie to kick to the curb. If you are giving it your best shot, then you are living a beautiful life.

## NUGGETS OF GOODNESS AND GRACE

Every once in a while, God gives us a little nugget of His goodness and grace. Mine often comes in the middle of the night as I hold a sleeping little one in my arms. It's then that I feel my heart fill with the warmest, sweetest joy and gratitude. It's in those quiet moments that I feel God telling me, "Keep going, Emily. Keep going. You're doing great."

> EVERY ONCE IN A WHILE, GOD GIVES US A LITTLE NUGGET OF HIS GOODNESS AND GRACE.

God uses small moments like these to give me a tiny bit of confidence to tuck away for the next time I need it. That's

## MY THOUGHTS

*Record all the good things you find in today.*

His grace. That's God giving me just what I need to keep going—even though I'm far from perfect.

God is dropping those nuggets of goodness and grace into your life too. Look for them. Search for them like the treasures they are. Maybe it's in a note from a teacher who's noticed how hard you're working. Maybe it's in a surprise cupcake from your mom on a tough day. Maybe it's in a hug from the child you helped at church. Or maybe it's the wonder of watching a sunset and knowing that the God who created that is watching over you.

WE LIVE TOO MANY DAYS WORRYING ABOUT WHETHER OR NOT WE'RE GOOD ENOUGH. STOP LISTENING TO THE LIES AND LISTEN TO GOD.

In those moments, I feel God telling me He loves me. And that I'm so very special to Him. Think about that for a minute. God loves you and cherishes you. He saves every piece of praise and artwork you create. He will watch you go down the slide a thousand times, even if He's busy. And He gives us little gifts of His goodness and grace to show us that He's with us. When God hands you one of those nuggets, hold on to it like a priceless treasure. And when the lies come knocking at your door, don't answer.

We live too many days worrying about whether or not we're good enough. Stop listening to the lies and listen to God.

# Chapter 14

# CHOOSE CONTENTMENT

Contentment: *a state of happiness and satisfaction*[1]

CONTENTMENT. IT BASICALLY MEANS BEING HAPPY with what we have. That's a tough concept for me. I tend to be more of a perfectionist—always searching for something better. Then one day my friend Nancy Ray shared her experience with a "contentment challenge." She was struggling with her need for more and more when she felt God leading her to put the brakes on her spending. So for ninety days she bought only the things she had to have, like peanut butter and toothpaste. This made room in her heart, home, and life for God to speak more clearly to her.

To me, that is what simplicity is all about. We're making

room for what matters. We're giving ourselves space to hear God more clearly, to give more wholeheartedly, and to pour our energy into people rather than in things. Simplifying allows us to slow down enough to savor this life.

We live in one of the richest societies in the world. So why do we want more when we have so much already? I feel uncomfortable even writing about it. Tens of thousands of people every day die from hunger. Yet we won't eat food just because it's not our favorite. Countless people around the world don't have good shoes to wear. But we're obsessed with getting just the right pair to match an outfit.

We have *so* much. We have education, food, shelter, technology, opportunities, abilities, and talents. But for some reason deep inside us, we still want more, better, faster, newer.

---

♥ Where do you see yourself wanting more and more? Keep track of your spending over the next week or two. Not just how you spend your money but also how you spend your time. What are you wasting the most time and money on? What hole might you be trying to fill?

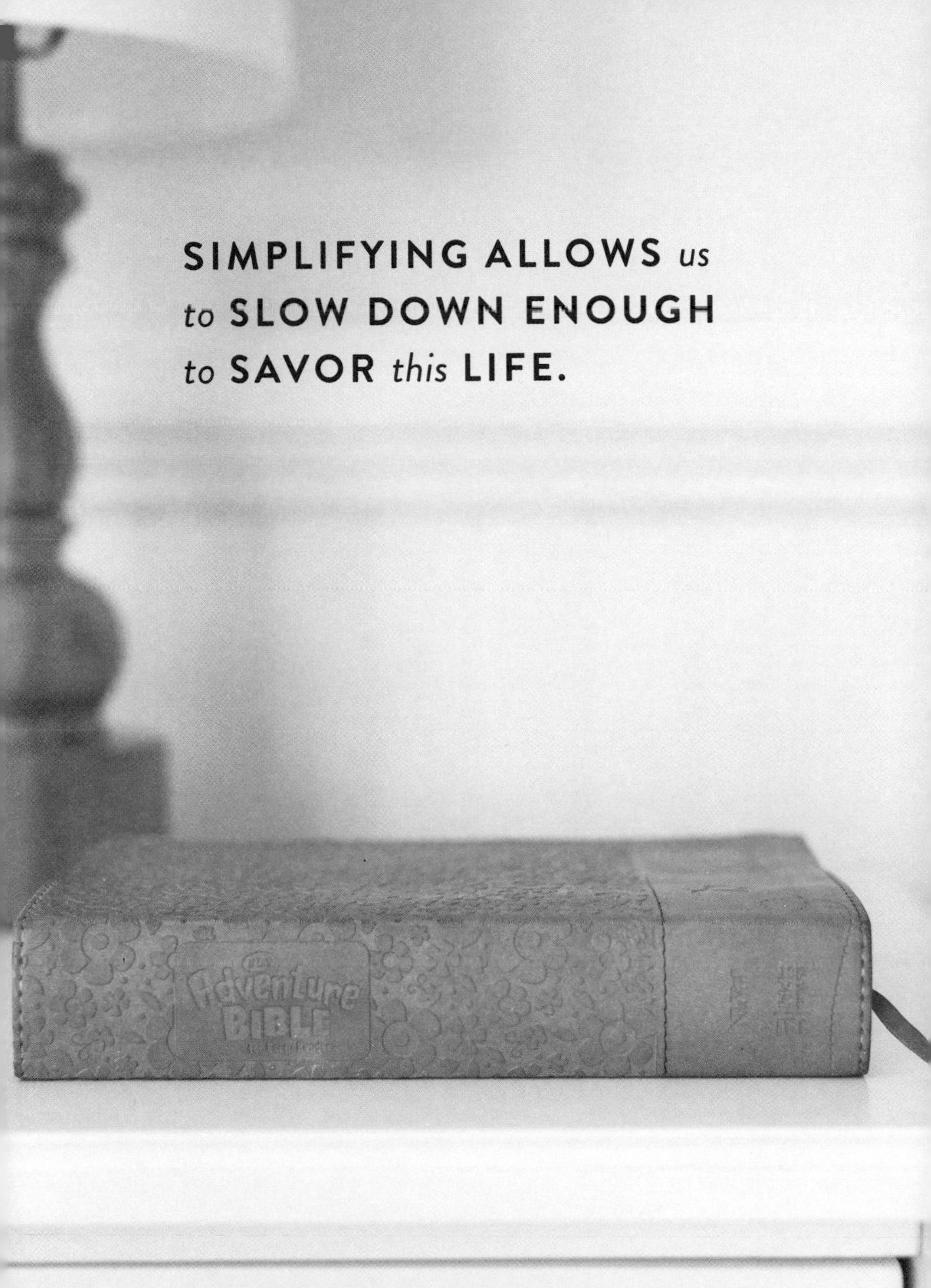
SIMPLIFYING ALLOWS *us*
*to* SLOW DOWN ENOUGH
*to* SAVOR *this* LIFE.
Adventure
BIBLE

We're always on the run. And we tell ourselves that's a good thing. But what if . . . what if we took a good look at the burning holes in our hearts to see what they are *really* shaped like? Is the hole we're filling really shaped like a new pair of shoes or a spot at the "popular" lunch table? We have to figure out what we're really aching for.

## SIMPLY CONTENT

Imagine what life would look like if we were truly content—truly happy—with what we already have. The word *content* means satisfied, and *satisfied* means pleased. Yes! I deeply want that kind of peace. To be content, satisfied, and pleased with my life and my stuff, just as it is. To not feel pushed to add more stuff to my space and more activities to my calendar. Because our lives could use more white space. More emptiness and more room to breathe. When we get rid of the excess, we make room for God.

## GETTING RID OF THE EXCESS

How do we get rid of excess? How do we find that feeling of contentment we're after? Our closets, bookshelves, and

*Chapter 15*

# LOVE YOUR LIFE *NOW*

*Embrace this season of life, for*
*it is just that . . . a season.*

THIS TIME IN YOUR LIFE IS JUST A SEASON. LIKE SPRING, summer, winter, or fall, this season will soon spill into the next. School—with all its drama and homework and stress—won't last forever. (Even if it feels like it will.) One day you really will be all grown up. But don't wish this season away. Grab hold of it. Squeeze every bit of joy and contentment out of it that you can. Don't be afraid to fully live every moment.

Sometimes living every moment—or at least the moments that really matter—means saying no. It might even mean saying no to good things. Because they aren't the best things for you.

DO *what* WORKS *for* YOU.
FORGET *the* REST.

be different will give someone else the permission, the inspiration, and the courage she needs to be true to herself too.

Find the things that fill your heart with joy and a sense of purpose—and then go for it. Define your own life. And if it doesn't look like what social media or the perfect girls say it should look like, then that's just fine. In fact, it's awesome. Do what works for you. Forget the rest.

Right now I'm sitting at my computer for the umpteenth night in a row, escaping my own little circus to write a book. And here at the end of it, I'm certain that my best advice to you is this: Soak it up. Dare to carve out your own life. Because that's where you'll find real joy. Just following the crowd will only lead you to "perfect," styled, and staged phony joy. *No thanks.*

> FIND THE THINGS THAT FILL YOUR HEART WITH JOY AND A SENSE OF PURPOSE—AND THEN GO FOR IT.

Be real. With yourself and with others. Don't let those bumps in the road stop you. Learn from them and keep going. Build structure and routine for your days, but build them with plenty of grace for those times when life gets crazy. Have real conversations with your parents and learn from their lives. Savor your friendships. They won't always be knocking your door down—or blowing up your phone—begging for a chance to talk. Make time. Make room. Make margin for what matters.

I have strong ideas about the type of life I want to live. Right now, though, I live with three small kiddos. That means my dream life is possible, but sometimes it's only in bits and pieces. Still, I have a goal I'm working toward. And God is changing my heart and challenging me as I work toward that goal. I know very well that He wants me—and you—to walk through this life with purpose and not skip along the path without thinking about who we are supposed to be. There are lessons and memories and stories to be found here, in this stage of life. Soak up every one you can get.

This stage of your life can be difficult. It may bring you to tears at times. You're right smack in the middle of figuring out who you are as a person and what you want your life now—and in the future—to look like. That's not easy. And while your dream life is possible, it may only be possible in bits and pieces at the moment.

> PERFECTION ISN'T EVEN POSSIBLE. LEARN TO LIVE AND LOVE IN THE MIDDLE OF IT.

God may be walking with you through some really tough times right now. Perhaps there are issues with friends or mean girls. Maybe there's illness or divorce or some other difficulty weighing you down. Some seasons are just plain hard. Grieve if you need to. Lean on your people—your family and your friends. Hold on to the joys of small pleasures. Sit in the sunshine. Hug your family and say, "I love you."

You only get this one life. Now is the time to live it. Not when you're grown up, and not when everything is "perfect." And here's a truth: perfection isn't even possible. Learn to live and love in the middle of all the imperfection. That's where the real joy is found. Use this time in your life to figure out what your gifts are, then let those gifts shine, and share them with the world.

## ONE DAY . . .

One day we'll add up all our seasons—the joyful ones, the heartbreaking ones, the over-the-top, average, and peaceful ones. When we do, we'll have one rich life story. It will be a picture of faith and doubt, grace and worry, friendship, learning, and loving. Each season connects to the next with a chain of growth and change. We'll look back at our experiences, and we'll have so many stories to tell. We'll tug out those treasured nuggets of goodness we've tucked away, and we'll pass on our wisdom to those who are younger. Sure, we may have scars from the countless times we face-planted in the dust, but we'll be really good at standing back up. And we can help others stand back up too. That, sweet friends, is what legacy is—the gifts we give to those who follow us.

What will your legacy be? What gifts will you share with those who are coming up behind you? Will your courage to be your own person help someone else do the same? Will the grace you give yourself and your people help others see the grace of God? When you pick yourself up from that epic face-plant, who will be watching and learning to carry on?

You have a gift right now. It's an opportunity to welcome

God's grace into your life. It's a chance to free yourself from the traps of this world's lies. Now is the time to tell yourself the truth:

You *are* measuring up.

You *are* doing just great.

You, *just as you are*, are enough.

Enough for yourself. Enough for God. And enough for the ones you love.

WHAT WILL YOUR LEGACY BE?

Here's one last exercise. Sit with your palms up and your eyes closed. Sit and dream for a moment. What story will you live? In many ways, you're just getting started. So many of your seasons are still to come. That next link in the chain is totally up to you. Is it grace? Trust? Faith? Growth? Choose your next step. The joy is found in the journey. It's a journey of simple and unending grace that is poured out on perfectly imperfect people like you and me. This is your time.

**YOU,**
***just as you are*,**
**ARE ENOUGH.**

# MY HOPE AND PRAYER FOR YOU

**DEAR FRIENDS,**

Every day is a gift. Open it up and live it.

Try new things. Learn and grow. Succeed and fail. And wear your skinned knees and your dirt proudly.

Explore. Dare. Dream. Figure out the passion God has planted in your heart. It's there, sweet girl. I promise. It's just waiting for you to uncover it.

Don't hide yourself away. Please stop worrying so much about what others will think. *Be you.* Beautiful, wonderful, amazing *you*. Because you are a gift God has created for this world. Don't let fear keep you from being that gift.

Stop chasing after the lie of perfection and instead fill those empty places in your heart with the truth of grace. The grace God gives you and the grace you give yourself.

Yes, this time of your life can be difficult. There will be

challenges and obstacles. There will be wounds and scars. But there will also be God. And He is working in your life for good.

Look for the joys, those nuggets of God's goodness and grace. Tuck them away and treasure them. Pull them out when you need to be reminded that you aren't ever in this life alone.

Find your place in God and His kingdom here on earth. Use the gifts He has given you to shine, to share His love and grace, and to make this world a better place.

xo,

Emily

# NOTES

## *Part 1: Give Yourself Some Grace*

1. *Merriam-Webster*, s.v. "tactical," accessed December 10, 2019, https://www.merriam-webster.com/dictionary/tactical.

## *Chapter 7: Enjoy the Circus*

1. *Merriam-Webster*, s.v. "three-ring circus," accessed December 11, 2019, https://www.merriam-webster.com/dictionary/three-ring%20circus.
2. André J. Szameitat, "A Neuroscientist Explains Why Multitasking Screens Is So Terrible for Your Brain," Science Alert, December 16, 2019, accessed December 17, 2019, https://www.sciencealert.com/multitasking-is-not-a-good-way-to-train-your-brain-here-s-why.

## *Chapter 14: Choose Contentment*

1. Lexico.com, s.v. "contentment," accessed December 12, 2019, https://www.lexico.com/definition/contentment.